Happy Land—A Lover's Revenge

Happy Land

—

A Lover's Revenge

The nightclub fire that shocked a nation

OJ Modjeska

Foreword

In the year 2019, as the American people looked around and surveyed what some might characterize as the detritus of a once great nation, many might be forgiven for thinking we have stumbled into an unprecedented age where up is down, the sky is not blue, and everything appears to be sliding in every direction.

In 2019, when people thought about mass murder, they thought about gun violence. For the nation was almost palpably awash with the blood of children murdered in schools, shoppers exterminated in supermarkets, and sports fans slain in stadiums by the angry, disenchanted, and lonesome: domestic terrorists armed with weapons under the continuing influence of that troublesome but hallowed Second Amendment.

Meanwhile, President Donald Trump was still talking about constructing a wall at the border with Mexico. The purported reason was to keep undesirables from Mexico and other equatorial zones out of America. There were those who thought that "the Donald" was not exactly a paragon of intellect, putting it kindly. But others suspected that there was more going on behind the scenes than was visible. Maybe he was cleverer—or at least more strategic—than he appeared? Trump was publicly a climate change denier. But what if he, or his advisors, knew that the wall had another, more important purpose? For while the children were being murdered in classrooms, the great migrations were beginning: the brown faces arriving in ever greater numbers, not because they were fleeing persecution in their homelands (although there was that) but because their crops were failing, they were running out of water and food, and they were dying in heat waves in record numbers. As the 2020s opened, the climate catastrophe had suddenly arrived—fully, visibly—and the equatorial world was approaching the brink of uninhabitability.

Climate change was little discussed in mainstream discourse as the reason "behind" things. People sometimes called it the elephant in the room. It had become impolite to mention at dinner parties and in workplaces. If you did that, you risked averted gazes and a rapid changing of the subject to something more pleasant like planned holidays and home improvement projects.

There was another elephant in the room, apart from the murdered and incarcerated children, the rapidly warming planet. Women were being killed by men—usually partners or former partners—in rapidly escalating and dizzying numbers. In the media, men who committed these crimes were usually characterized as mentally ill or aberrant, much like the gun-toting maniacs who killed the school kids. But for thoughtful and curious observers, it was hard to conclude that there wasn't something more systemic going on underneath.

And what if it was all related? The shooting of the children, the killing of women, the refugees camped at the borders? Well, it is, and was. The common denominator is the rage and desperation of planetary occupants who feel disinherited and deprived of what they believe was once, rightly or wrongfully, theirs, whether their lands, their women, or the mythologized racial purity of past communities.

Which brings us to the subject of this book.

For while it is tempting to conclude that this is indeed a new world in which old rules no longer apply—"uncharted territory"—there is, in fact, little that is completely new under the sun. At least, historians (a profession of which this author is a member) know that the antecedents to a terrifying and seemingly unfamiliar present can always be located in the past.

* * *

The phenomenon of mass murder is generally understood as the act of killing a number of people, typically simultaneously or over a relatively short period of time and in close geographic proximity. As mentioned, Americans today tend to think of mass murder in terms of mass shootings. At the time of writing, the deadliest example of that occurred in Las Vegas in 2017, with 58 killed but an incredible 851 injured.

It may come as a surprise, then, that less than thirty years ago, in 1990, the worst mass murder in American history to date was not carried out by a gunman but an arsonist.

The Happy Land nightclub fire, which occurred on March 25, 1990, in the West Bronx, claimed 87 victims—at that time the largest death toll from a single-perpetrator act of violence occurring in a single incident.

As deadly as it was, the fire is little remembered today outside the community that it directly affected. However, for this author personally, it is sometimes history's little known and remembered events that offer the most compelling curiosity.

Such was the case with Happy Land when I began to research the tragedy in detail. What initially appeared to be an obscure incident from the past turned out to contain an amazing story with rich contemporary resonance.

The story had three achingly familiar, overlapping plotlines: a man rejected by a woman who visited a terrible act of violence on innocent people as revenge. Immigrants who left their homelands in search of survival and livelihood and found themselves largely unwelcome and on the periphery in their new country. Humans ill-equipped to face epic disasters in the face of public indifference and crumbling infrastructure.

None of these things are new. But there is a surprising element to the Happy Land story too. In a way, it offers a look back into a more compassionate and authentic time and provides a blistering sense of how much our society has changed, and how quickly—not necessarily for the better. In the years since the Happy Land fire occurred, the significance of the tragedy for most Americans has been gradually eclipsed by a monotonous series of mass killings that have happened since, many on a larger scale—such as 9/11, in which 2,977 people lost their lives. Today, people are constantly suffering and dying in lands both close and distant, and nobody as much as bats an eyelid: for this is our new "normal," where apathy, compassion fatigue and an overriding sense of defeat have settled into our hearts. No longer do limitless resources and a narrative of a benign and progressive future support our efforts to have empathy for the most vulnerable in our midst—those who get the short end in the relentless march of development and consumption.

But at the time, this disaster and its attendant stories, beamed via TV sets into white middle-class homes all over the country, seized and appalled the public imagination. And by virtue of the fact that this was the worst mass murder in

American history, ordinary Americans everywhere were about to get an eye-opening glimpse into a world they hitherto knew—and thought—little about.

Back in the eighties and nineties, everyone was accustomed to hearing about "fire in the Bronx." The borough, afflicted for years by poverty and urban decay, had been almost permanently alight throughout the seventies, when landlords burned down their own properties to collect insurance monies for unsaleable and abandoned buildings. So routine had these fires become that nobody thought much of it. But this fire was different, and what was different about it cast a spotlight on the inner life and complexities of a Bronx neighborhood, and the struggles of its inhabitants, in a way that was unprecedented—and rather shocking.

It was maybe the Bronx's most devastating tragedy. Even today, the fire summons recollections that are so personal and painful for so many residents. Thirty years has not been enough to erase the memories of horror, and perhaps no amount of time ever will be.

And even today the people of East Tremont have never forgotten the hatred and rage they felt against the man responsible, while others have not forgotten their resentment towards the woman whose rejection inspired his horrific act of violence.

Even so, perhaps what is so remarkable about the Happy Land story stands in contrast to the very intense feelings it arouses in the people it affected. It is a tale that is appalling—and yet also troublingly ordinary.

A typical crime story has easily identifiable villains and victims. This story is of another kind— and it is grim, fascinating and unspeakably sad, in large part because it is a tale where all the protagonists, both the perpetrator and the victims, were caught in similar realms of suffering and disadvantage. Crime movies and novels featuring the old trope of super villains getting their due are gratifying to humanity's fears and delusions about the nature of evil. In real life, however, terrible acts of cruelty and violence often spring from the limits to human tolerance for the mundane pains and struggles inflicted on people by the society in which they live. Happy Land is such a story.

Those who lived through the fire passed the tale to their children, and the Happy Land story became legendary in the Bronx, part of its urban folklore.

It is this author's contention that it should not be forgotten by the world.

Chapter 1

In New York's outer suburban rings in the small hours of March 25, 1990, all was quiet, with most residents tucked up asleep in their beds. Meanwhile the streets of East Tremont, the Bronx, were alive with noise, traffic and colorfully clad locals who had no intention of retiring any time soon.

March 25 is the annual date of *Punta Carnivale*, the equivalent of Mardi Gras in Central America. So it was that even at 3 a.m., the streets thronged with Hispanic and Caribbean revelers, many of whom were spilling out of local nightclubs to head home or continue their fun at other establishments.

The neighborhood, decayed and desperate, was rarely given a thought or a glance by white middle-class New Yorkers—except when there was some kind of crackdown going on. The spectral West Bronx skyline was haunted by the shadows of abandoned buildings, and nestled between them were empty lots strewn with sundry trash—busted pallets, crushed bottles, dirty and torn mattresses, burned-out vehicles. Photographs from the time show a city more resembling Kosovo or Beirut than any image we generally associate with New York, New York.

The area had been through many social and economic transformations since the second world war; mid-century it was home primarily to Irish and Italian immigrants, but by the sixties it had evolved into an African American community, and in the seventies and eighties the black locals were joined by large numbers of immigrants from Puerto Rico, Honduras, Ecuador and Mexico.

Most of the time, as soon as the Central Americans landed in New York, they already knew where they were going. They headed straight to the Bronx—where they would find others like themselves, and where they wouldn't bother the white folks.

And life in East Tremont wasn't all bad. Boom boxes playing hip-hop and reggae on corners, street vendors selling colorful curiosities and home crafts, cafes that served homestyle Latin and Caribbean food. And then, after dark, the people would forget their troubles and their straitened circumstances at the clubs that lined the streets of Southern Boulevard and East Tremont Avenue, which served cheap alcoholic drinks and charged no or low entry fees, often around five dollars.

One such club was Happy Land, a small but popular nightspot which occupied an unassuming building located on Southern Boulevard, partway between the intersections of Crotona Parkway and East Tremont Avenue.

Shortly after 3:30 a.m. on the night of *Punta Carnivale*, pedestrians in the area smelled heavy plumes of smoke. Those passing through Southern Boulevard saw that the entire facade of the building located at 1959 was on fire. A local resident who was out and about for the celebrations rushed to a payphone and dialed the fire department.

At 3:41 a.m., just minutes after the blaze erupted, officers of the FDNY arrived at the scene.

As the firefighters hosed the entry and hallway of the club, on the steps they saw several charred bodies. The victims, Black and Hispanic immigrants in their late teens and early twenties, were piled towards the door; these people had been stampeding for the fire-enveloped exit... which raised the possibility that the blazing doorway had been the only way in our out.

More bodies were scattered on the first-floor bar room floor. The men began pulling these victims on the first floor out one by one. Their number soon reached nineteen; this was very bad, but not as bad as it could be, they told themselves. Fires happened in the Bronx all the time. Such incidents as this had become sadly commonplace over the years.

But they had yet to discover the scene on the second floor. The men began to ascend the steps of the narrow wooden staircase in single file. As they emerged into the darkened room, they noticed a strange feeling under their feet. There were piles of stuff on the ground; clothing and discarded purses and other personal effects.

But that wasn't all. No, it wasn't just clothing they were tripping over. They were standing and stepping on bodies.

One of the officers let out an anguished cry.

Oh, no...

The room—small, dim and windowless—was packed with dead bodies. Everywhere the men pointed their flashlights, they saw bodies, piled one on top of the other. In some areas, the bodies were piled four deep.

Once the room was cleared of smoke, the full horror was revealed, so terrible that some of the men vomited. The club had been filled with underaged kids. Many of the victims were little girls, teenagers, dressed in their best party clothes.

Their bodies were not burnt in the slightest. They had died long before the fire could reach them. They had seemingly died in seconds, not minutes. Gas or asphyxiation had claimed them at an unfathomable speed.

Some had died still clutching their glasses. They had died seated at tables. They had died clawing at their throats.

"The scene was paralyzing," FDNY Assistant Chief Frank Nastro later said. "We stood there numbed. No one spoke. There were 69 bodies spread about this 24-by-50-foot area. They all could have been sleeping."

Later, when questioned by the press, the firemen would strain to find appropriate analogies for the surreal scene of carnage. For while a fire had surely taken the victims, these did not look like any fire victims they were used to seeing—and many of the men, confronted with what appeared more like a room stuffed with mannequins, wondered how it could even happen.

Pompeii. Hiroshima. A Nazi gas chamber, were some of the words they used.

Sixty-nine bodies in a single small room, frozen in time.

Chapter 2

The detectives and firemen who gathered at the scene quickly surmised a couple of important facts about the fire.

The first was that Happy Land, like many similar clubs around the Bronx, was an illegal operation and had been housed inside a building lacking relevant permits and patently unfit for occupation. Such was part of the explanation for the scene of horror on the second floor, a small windowless room packed well beyond its capacity, that had been rapidly drained of oxygen as the fire approached from the floor below, suffocating everyone inside.

These people shouldn't have been here, an officer remarked.

Which kind of begged the question—where *should* they have been?

It was an old problem. Immigrants from Central America came to the United States looking for livelihood and a better existence. Some secured residential rights, others were illegals. They flooded the Bronx, looking for the companionship of congenial relatives and friends, and found themselves on the margins of New York life. Packed into crumbling and unsafe tenements and into illegal and dangerous nightclubs… for these were the places they could afford and could find welcome. Just some years back there had been a fire at a similar nightclub, El Hoyo. The victims had been young immigrants, just like these ones. Luckily only seven, on that occasion.

It was also clear to the detectives that, despite the fact that the building was a firetrap and an accident waiting to happen, the fire at Happy Land had been no mishap. The entryway to the club was pervaded by a smell of gasoline. Then, they found an empty plastic Blackhawk gasoline container on the street, not far from the club's entrance. They were dealing with arson. And it looked as though whoever had done it was perhaps not too concerned about getting caught.

It was possible that the arson had been a random attack—executed by a crazed passer-by or a patron, someone engaged in destruction for its own sake—but first instincts didn't tell them so. Nor was it likely the crime had a pecuniary motive such as people were used to seeing in the Bronx—building owners who set fire to their property to collect insurance money. If that were the case, why had a fire been lit when the building was packed with partygoers?

Instead, they were forming an impression that a deliberate act of violence had taken place—an act of aggression against the club, its owners or operators, or somebody who worked there or frequented the place regularly.

Their suspicions would be confirmed within hours. A Puerto Rican woman in her early forties named Lydia Feliciano came into the precinct and told Detective Andrew Lugo, who spoke her native Spanish, that she was an employee of the club and had been there the night before when the fire broke out. She had managed to escape with three other people—she wasn't sure how many other survivors there might be.

The thing was, she had an inkling that the fire might have been set by her ex-boyfriend. He had come to the club the night before seeking reconciliation. There had been some trouble, an argument, and the bouncer had thrown him out. The fire engulfed the entryway a short time later.

Of course, she couldn't be completely sure he was responsible. But the timing was very suspicious.

Detectives pulled up the suspect's information and discovered that, like most of his victims (assuming he was the man responsible), he too was an immigrant from Central America—a Cuban who had come to America on the Mariel boatlift in 1980.

He wasn't an illegal but a so-called "parolee," a designation given to immigrants released from detention centers who had neither citizenship nor residential status but were allowed to remain in the United States as long as they never committed a crime.

And it appeared from his record that, up until the present time, he hadn't—at least not one that was documented.

Chapter 3

So far, the man's name and the fact that he was a *Marielito* was about all the police knew about their lead suspect.

The latter point set bells ringing slightly, whether unfairly or not. There was a great deal of prejudice towards the *Marielitos* within the United States. Thanks in part to the 1983 film *Scarface* and its depiction of Tony Montana, the violent drug kingpin of Miami, they had become one of the most feared and reviled immigrant groups in the United States.

Based on Feliciano's description, the officers weren't expecting to find a Tony Montana in their suspect. Still, his background concerned them.

It wasn't just a matter of ordinary prejudice. It wasn't just the layers and layers of white resentment about the recent influx of immigrants from southern nations, some illegal, some with "illegitimate" claims to asylum, some with obvious bad intentions, some who might be violent, mad or out-of-control... although there was all that, too, that accounted for public sentiment towards *Marielitos*.

The man at the center of the case would indeed become another poster child for conservative commentators who decried the dangers to American society of new arrivals from nations with incongruous mores and values. But the story behind the Mariel boat people had an additional specific dimension to it that terrified and infuriated many American people. In their narrative, no group of immigrants could be more illegitimate or more frightening than this one, for these were the people Castro had unleashed on America for revenge.

American life had already been fractured for many decades by debates about the possible negative effects of immigration on the homeland. The American Dream has always held forth the idea that those coming from distant shores have a positive contribution to make to society and in return may themselves be enriched by economic opportunity and the possibility of a better life. Critics, however, have always been at pains to point out that "we don't really know who these people are." Good intentions aside, they say, are we not inviting terrorists, criminals, drug dealers and murderers into our borders along with those small handfuls of folk who "have a positive contribution to make to society"?

The debate is further complicated when, over time, both left and right have tended to agree on America's obligation to provide safe haven for victims of enemy regimes. Isolationist skeptics contend such soft-hearted idealism is misguided and dangerous, a foolish by-product of America's arrogant belief in its own moral superiority. *We are better than them—it is our responsibility to help them!*

Such claims were made about the Mariel boatlift of 1980, during which some 125,000 Cuban nationals escaped Fidel Castro's regime by agreement between the Jimmy Carter administration and the Cuban government. The agreement was terminated in late October 1980 after the influx of *Marielitos* began to pose a political problem for the Carter administration; it turned out that many of these promising immigrants were convicted criminals or mentally ill. The American people naturally did not like this.

Certainly Fidel Castro was one who thought America's philosophy of "lending a hand to their lessors" was condescending and offensive. His actions in response proved him to be a man with a rather wry sense of humor. Jimmy Carter was a president whose well-intentioned nature history would cast in the light of weakness. In this instance his bleeding heart and hand-wringing was exploited for all it was worth, and he would be judged harshly for it.

Carter's administration had been seeking rapprochement with the Cuban government for some years, in part due to a desire to relax trade embargos. In the late seventies, after many harsh years of economic austerity under the regime, thousands of Cuban asylum seekers sought refuge in South American embassies, provoking a crisis for the Cuban government that reached its apex in April 1980. Following the offer of the deal welcoming refugees by the American government, Castro announced that the port of Mariel would be opened to anyone wishing to leave Cuba, as long as they had someone to pick them up. Most of the *Marielitos* who took advantage of the offer were indeed ordinary citizens seeking asylum. But in a move inspired by vindictiveness on the part of Castro, who resented the official American welcome, the regime emptied several of its jails and mental hospitals and sent those freed to Mariel Bay, ensuring that the Americans would get far more than they bargained for—and discouraging a repeat of any such generosity in future.

One of these "victims of the regime" who would embark on the freedom flotilla to the USA was a man named Julio Gonzalez.

Chapter 4

On the morning of March 25 at around 5:00a.m., Lieutenant James Malvey, commanding officer of the 48th Precinct Detective Squad, was informed by a police dispatcher that more than 80 people had died in a fire at the Happy Land Social Club on Southern Boulevard.

Malvey dressed and headed to the precinct and briefed Detective Kevin Moroney with the little information at that time available and assigned him to the case.

"I was doing a turnaround that night," Moroney later said. "[Malvey] came running into my office and yelled that eighty people were killed in a fire. My first reaction was, what the hell is he talking about? I never heard of such a thing; I didn't believe it at first."

Within moments, the precinct foyer was enveloped in chaos as the press, local district attorneys, fire department and Emergency Medical Services (EMS) representatives and police officers descended on the building, demanding an audience for their questions or critical information they had to pass on. Malvey and Moroney rushed to 1959 Southern Boulevard and found a similar scene of disorder there, the pavement crowded with near-hysterical friends and relatives wanting to know the whereabouts of loved ones. At this time they found the gas canister outside.

Upon returning to the precinct, Moroney spoke to Andrew Lugo and learned that Lydia Feliciano had given him a statement implicating her ex-boyfriend Julio Gonzalez. She had told Detective Lugo that Gonzalez had arrived at the club around 3:00am. The former lovers had quarreled and before being removed by the bouncer, Gonzalez had angrily told Feliciano, "You'll see. Tomorrow you're not going to be working here." Additionally, Ms. Feliciano told Lugo that her niece had seen Gonzalez outside the club at approximately 3:30am—right before the fire broke out.

By this time the officers were pretty confident they had a lead on the right suspect. But Moroney decided he wanted to talk to Feliciano directly before they made a move. He was told by the precinct that he would find her at the temporary morgue set up at Public School 57 for the identification of victims, as she was going there to seek information on the whereabouts of her niece.

The scene at Public School 57 at 2111 Crotona Avenue was truly awful to behold. There a large, emotional crowd had gathered, waiting to find out if their loved ones were amongst the victims. With so many victims, everyone knew that if they knew someone who had gone to the club that night, there was a good chance they were dead. Wails, screams and sobs were heard regularly erupting from the congregation of mourners as one by one, the people received confirmation of their worst fears.

Detective Moroney soon located Feliciano, who had sadly found what she was looking for: a photograph of her niece Betsy Torres. Betsy had been upstairs at Happy Land, and she was one of those who had died in such a horrific way.

Feliciano repeated her information about the altercation with Gonzalez the night previous: the fact that he had been ejected from the club and had made threats to "come back" and "close the place down".

When Moroney asked Feliciano if she thought Gonzalez could have set the fire, she told Moroney that if he had asked her the same question several months ago, she would have said no. She just didn't think he was that type of guy. He was quiet, and gentle. But after she broke up with Gonzalez, she saw a side to him that had apparently remained hidden for the duration of their relationship.

He had been broken, humiliated and enraged beyond measure by her rejection. In his mind, Feliciano had no business leaving him. She belonged to him. He had ranted at the bouncer, "she's my woman, not yours!"

And Gonzalez was morbidly jealous, imagining that in his absence she was taking up with any man that frequented the club.

Yes, she said, Gonzalez could have done it. In fact, she felt that he must have done it.

* * *

All other things being equal, if Gonzalez had set the fire, there was a good chance he had already disappeared. He had had a clear window to make a get-away. They might never find the man responsible.

But another important piece of information arrived at the precinct that morning. A man named Arturo Martinez, who described himself as a friend of Gonzalez, told detectives Gonzalez had definitely set the fire, that he could show them where the suspect lived, and that they would find him at home.

The reason he was so sure about that was because he had spoken to Gonzalez earlier in the day. He said he had placed a call to Gonzalez at about 9:30 that morning, wanting to ask him about the fire, but was told he was asleep.

Asleep? The officers glanced at each other, bemused. The man who had set the fire had gone home and gone to sleep?

Gonzalez never went on the run. Instead, he got out of bed briefly to call Martinez back. At the time, in response to Martinez's enquiry, Gonzalez denied setting the club alight. Gonzalez would later tell detectives he had denied his role because he didn't want to discuss it with Martinez over the phone. At around 11:30a.m. that day, Martinez went to Gonzalez's residence and spoke to Gonzalez while the two sat in Martinez's car. Martinez told Gonzalez that Feliciano had survived the fire and that she would tell the police what she knew, if she hadn't already; and it was thus inevitable he would be charged. In response, Gonzalez told his friend that if the police came around asking questions, Martinez should "tell the truth" and give them his address because he was going to surrender.

That afternoon, Detective Andrew Lugo, Lieutenant Malvey, and Detective Moroney proceeded in an unmarked vehicle to 31 Buchanan Place in the University Heights area, the suspect's address since he had been ejected from Lydia Feliciano's apartment some five weeks earlier.

At around 2:00p.m., Detective Lugo and the other officers entered the building and ascended one flight of stairs. None of the men were wearing bullet-proof vests, because by this time, no trouble from the suspect was expected.

On the landing, they encountered Pedro Rivera and Carmen Melendez, neighbors of Gonzalez at the boarding house at 31 Buchanan Place. They informed the detectives that Gonzalez was upstairs in bed.

He was *still* asleep. Gonzalez had apparently been sleeping on and off all day, getting out of bed briefly to attend to the calls and visit from his friend, and then returning to bed.

Carmen Melendez told the officers that in the early hours of the morning, Julio Gonzalez had knocked on her door. She had let him into their room and Gonzalez had collapsed at the foot of her bed, wailing like a baby. In between sobs he said that he had burned down the club and killed Feliciano. But Carmen didn't believe him. She thought he was drunk and telling stories. She told him to go upstairs and sleep it off—which was apparently exactly what he did.

The detectives also exchanged words with the owner of the rooming house, John O'Keefe, who said that Gonzalez was out of work and weeks behind on rent.

"From what I know," he said, "he was down to his last hope."

At Detective Lugo's request, Mr. Rivera went ahead of them up the stairs and knocked on Gonzalez's door.

"Julio!" Rivera said as he knocked on the door.

"Si," Gonzalez replied through the door. Shortly after, Gonzalez—a small, thin, unremarkable looking man—opened it and stood there bleary-eyed, attired only in a shirt and pants.

As soon as the door was opened, the detectives were immediately bowled over by the overpowering odor of gasoline. They now were practically assured that they had their man.

Detective Lugo showed his police badge and identification card to the suspect, and the latter, without being asked, said "yes, come in" and gestured a welcome with his right hand.

Lugo was fluent in Spanish, so he conducted the preliminary conversations with the suspect while the other officers hung back.

Looking around the room, Detective Moroney observed a carry bag and other personal effects scattered in open view on some furniture. The suspect apparently wasn't making any effort to conceal his possessions or activities and hadn't been planning on going anywhere. If, as the exchange with Martinez had implied, he had at one time contemplated escaping or denying his involvement, that time was well past.

Despite the horrific scene at Happy Land, the detectives were troubled by a strange and unexpected feeling as they surveyed the tiny room and its contents. Room Number 7 contained a sink, a small refrigerator and a hot plate. In the cabinet were a few mugs, some shaving items and an empty beer bottle wrapped in a paper bag. There were very few garments in the closet.

O'Keefe had told them that Gonzalez had been unemployed for some time and was surviving by hustling on the streets. They were standing in the desolate home of an impoverished drifter; it had no warmth or personality, no sense of comfort. There, the desperation and futility of the occupant's life was almost palpable. The men were forming the impression that Gonzalez had hoped and believed beyond all reason that he was going back to Feliciano—for certainly, it didn't look like he planned on staying here; not for long anyway. And if Feliciano wasn't going to take him back, he had no other plan—none except, perhaps, the awfully destructive one he had ended up carrying out.

In a mild and conversational tone, Detective Lugo asked Gonzalez if he would come with them to the station to discuss an active investigation, without disclosing what the subject of the investigation was. Gonzalez immediately agreed, saying "yes, let's go."

It was cold out, and Gonzalez put on a maroon-colored jacket in preparation for leaving. Detective Lugo, concerned about the gasoline on Gonzalez's shoes, asked if he had an alternative pair he might put on. Gonzalez said that he didn't have another pair of shoes. He put the gasoline soaked black shoes on and silently went ahead of the others out of the room and down the stairs. They did not need to touch, cuff, or restrain him.

There was no talk during the ride to the precinct, but for a request by Gonzalez to smoke a cigarette, which was denied because of the risk posed by the gasoline on his shoes. The night previous he had set fire to a club and killed 87 people. Astonishingly, he still wasn't worried about starting a fire.

At the four-eight, once Gonzalez had been sequestered in the interview room, he was offered coffee which he gratefully accepted. While Detective Moroney went to fetch the refreshments, Detective Lugo remarked to Gonzalez that the investigation in relation to which he was being questioned was a fire at the Happy Land Social Club, and it was his understanding that Gonzalez had been there the night before.

Gonzalez, with no further prompting, burst into tears. He put his face in his hands and his head to his knees.

"It was me", he said. "I did it. I set fire to the club."

"We pretty much didn't even need to ask him anything," Moroney commented later.

Once having been read his Miranda rights in Spanish, Gonzalez voluntarily made an oral statement taking responsibility for the arson attack.

And then, the whole terrible story came out.

Chapter 5

Julio Gonzalez was born on 10 October 1954 in Holguín, a city in Oriente Province in Cuba, famed as the location of Christopher Columbus's arrival in the new world in 1492. Holguin, a coastal city, is also known for its tourist resorts and beaches, but Gonzalez came from an impoverished and far less attractive inner district of the town.

In May 1980, he was just 26 years old, and had already spent a decent chunk of his hard-scrabble life behind bars. But he was not a criminal in the sense most people think of it. As far as anyone knows, he hadn't killed anyone—yet.

Instead he had landed in jail after deserting the Cuban army—which was indeed a very serious offence in that place and time, where military service was compulsory, and Cuba was engaged in multiple conflicts as a result of its policy of proletarian internationalism, which emphasized providing direct military assistance to friendly governments and resistance movements worldwide.

He was released after three years, but not long after, he decided that he wanted to go back to prison. Outwardly the decision seems peculiar, but there was a logic to it beyond standard recidivism. He had heard rumors from his countrymen that the government were releasing people convicted of serious criminal offences from prison and sending them on boats to the United States.

It sounded crazy. Why would Castro round up criminals from his jails, let them out when they hadn't served out their sentences, and then reward them with passage to the United States? But that, people told him, was exactly what was happening.

In April of 1980 Gonzalez heard the tales from the frontlines of an exploding crisis. Cuban asylum seekers crashed a bus through the gates of the Peruvian embassy. People just like him, people who were desperate to leave after years of a stagnating economy, food shortages, housing shortages.

The Cuban Communist Party staged meetings at the homes of those known to be intending to leave the country, or even those just suspected of planning to go. At these "repudiation meetings" (*mitines de repudio*), party stooges and sympathetic citizens screamed obscenities and defiled the facades of homes with eggs and garbage. Labeled as "traitors to the revolution", those who declared their wish to abandon Cuba became the targeted victims of the attacks, their rationing cards taken, their jobs terminated, their enrolments at schools and universities cancelled.

Meanwhile, some Cubans had returned to the island from America, bringing money, shiny appliances and tales of a life of comparative freedom, wealth and privilege. Now everyone wanted a piece of that.

At the embassy, the Cuban guards opened fire on the asylum seekers. They killed their own people, rather than allow them to leave. Castro demanded the release of the exiles to the Cuban government, but the Peruvians refused.

And then, a stunning about-face. Castro had apparently thrown up his hands. He removed the guards from the Embassy, leaving it unprotected. Within hours, over 10,000 Cubans had stormed the grounds demanding protection. Castro agreed to allow the asylum seekers to leave. And on 20 April 1980 Castro declared that anyone who wanted to leave Cuba was free to do so, as long as they left via the Mariel Harbor.

But Castro had not thrown up his hands. His strategy was thought-out and intentional. Suddenly he was happy to rid his country of these people. They were disloyal undesirables, human trash. He reframed his loss as a victory: a cleansing and purifying purge of his great nation.

The radical change of tune, of course, was accounted for by something the Americans could not see. Something that would be visited on them in the form of dark future events, and sinister visitors. Men like Julio Gonzalez.

* * *

Gonzalez was tired of the army, tired of his poverty and aimlessness, and tired of Cuba. He was married, but he hadn't seen his wife for years, and didn't even know where she was. He had eloped with her on impulse one night after he was late bringing her home from a party. That, and no other reason, was why they had been wed. He had a young daughter, but there was nothing he could give to her.

He had nowhere to go and nothing to do. He was a man who had never really had anything in life, and a man with nothing is also a man with nothing to lose.

He decided to get himself one of those one-way tickets to America. He went to the authorities and handed himself over for a fictitious crime, voluntarily signing a confession to drug trafficking.

On 15 May 1980, he was languishing in the tropical heat of his cell on what appeared to be just another day, when he heard the guards yelling. He heard commotion, the shuffling of feet, and the clanging of cell doors. He looked into the hallway and saw that the long-awaited exodus was taking place. The guards weren't just letting the prisoners out, they were booting the men out of the cells, and prodding them out into the world with the barrels of their rifles.

Soon, he was one of the men scooped up and ejected beyond the prison walls, a rifle in his back. The guards led them on a long, sweaty march through the forest that eventually terminated on the sandy shores of Mariel Bay, home of the Cuban port closest to the United States.

The vast bay, with its port, factories, and power station, was dirty and noisy rather than idyllic, as tropical bays are often imagined to be. The sand, grey with contamination, crunched under the soles of their boots as they walked, and the sun beat down on their backs with an immovable fury.

Nearly seventy years earlier, a young Cuban named Agustin Parla, born to parents exiled during Cuba's struggle for independence, made the first flight from Key West, Florida to Mariel on 19 May 1913. Now, hundreds of Cubans, voluntary exiles, were waiting to cross the seas in the opposite direction to the United States. But they would not be flying; they would travel by boat.

Gonzalez huddled inconspicuously amongst his fellow prisoners—thieves, rapists, killers, and drug dealers such as he himself purported to be—on the beach. Together they sat quietly and waited for something to happen.

In the distance he saw small, fragile boats lumbering under the weight of their human cargo, which seemed to be almost spilling over the decks. One by one they disappeared over the horizon. Were they really destined for America? Was he going to America? He didn't know and he didn't really care. Anywhere was better than where he had been. In the prison, he went days without eating. In America, he would probably eat better out of a trash can.

Soon, the guards were on the move again. "Vamonos! Rapido!" ("Move along! Quick!") they shouted, jabbing the prisoners' backs with their guns. The cohort of undesirables were marshalled onto a decaying wooden deck that creaked alarmingly under the weight of hundreds of people, and from there, shoved into boats much like the ones Gonzalez had seen leaving the bay—barely seaworthy grails of promise.

The heat was relentless, and the overstuffed vessels lurched and groaned perilously in the waves of the Florida straits.

Some of the boats never made it across; they capsized and sank in the churning ocean, and those on board were never seen again. Eaten by sharks, the *Marielitos* said.

But Julio Gonzalez's boat was not one of these. He landed safely at Key West on 31 May 1980.

At the end of the jetty was a large, shining vending machine packed with cans of Coca-Cola. He had arrived in America.

* * *

For the *Marielitos* who were fortunate enough to make safe passage during the months of the Mariel boatlift between 15 April and 31 October 1980, a new ordeal awaited them in the United States.

Julio Gonzalez was one of the many who found themselves immediately detained again upon arrival. Makeshift refugee processing centers had been set up in Key West, Opa-Locka and Miami. Once initially processed and documented, the refugees would be moved to larger compounds in the metropolitan area so they could be reunited with relatives already living in the United States, where possible. Agencies such as Catholic Charities and the American Red Cross also visited the compounds to organize financial and legal aid.

Conditions in the South Florida processing centers became intolerably overcrowded with the continuing influx of refugees, and as a result, many were transferred to new "holding" centers in Arkansas, Pennsylvania and Wisconsin. "Hard to sponsor" refugees, which included those with criminal records, such as Gonzalez, were also sent for longer-term processing to these sites at Fort Chaffee, Fort Indiantown Gap, and Fort McCoy.

Cuban refugees rioted and staged hunger strikes in some centers due to the overcrowding, harsh conditions and delays in processing. Significant numbers of *Marielitos* had some kind of mental or physical illness but were not receiving any adequate medical treatment. Violent assaults and suicides were common occurrences. Allegations of brutality or torture by U.S. soldiers and guards occasionally appeared in the press; at Fort Chaffee, five guards were indicted over charges of beating refugees, but no one was ever convicted because of these allegations.

Lula Rodríguez, sister-in-law of then Hialeah mayor Raúl Martínez, worked as a volunteer in the refugee processing camps. She said that the plight of many Mariel refugees was seared in her memory and that the exodus made her realize just how terrible the Castro regime was.

"I saw people who were taken from mental hospitals," Rodríguez recalled in an interview. "Many of them were dazed. They asked questions like 'when is the doctor going to see me?' They were not even aware that they were in another country. That's when I realized the monstrosity of Fidel Castro."

Gonzalez was detained by U.S. immigration officials at Camp McCoy, Wisconsin, and Fort Chaffee, Arkansas, until his release on 21 February 1981. Nobody knows for sure what he saw or experienced while in detention. Regardless, eventually he was freed, bringing an almost incomprehensible lifetime of experiences with him to New York, where he finally settled by the winter of 1981.

Verne Jervis of the Immigration and Naturalization Service in Washington said Gonzalez was granted parolee status in 1981 and went to live with a sponsor family in New York City, adding, "We've had no contact from him since."

By the winter of 1981 he was living and working in Manhattan under the sponsorship of the American Council for Nationalities. His sponsor was one Juana Acosta, an immigrant from Santo Domingo, Dominican Republic.

Ms. Acosta was always wistful in her remembrances of Julio, her "boy", the kindly and shy lost one who landed on her doorstep and fell gratefully into her arms.

She described herself to press and detectives as Gonzalez's "adoptive mother". Indeed, his nickname for her was "mama". All this implies that she got to know Gonzalez very well. However, based on her characterization of him, it isn't clear how well she knew him at all.

Gonzales, she said, was very quiet. In fact, "he only spoke when spoken to". Nonetheless she thought highly of him, describing him as calm and helpful. Acosta sponsored six other Cubans who had come on the Mariel float. But her "boy", Gonzalez, was "the best of all". He was a model housemate, she said, regularly helping her with grocery shopping, never arguing and "never coming home drunk".

No matter what Gonzalez had done, Acosta said, she would always love and care for him. No matter what people said about him, that he was a "monster"—like the press called him, in giant black block letters splashed across the front of the papers—she could never accept that he was really a bad man. He was a good boy, with a hurting soul. He was a poor, lost thing. He just never really had a chance in life.

Under the sponsorship arrangement, Gonzalez lived with Acosta in her apartment in East Harlem for roughly two years between 1982 and 1984. In this period he also found employment at a lamp factory in Queens, packing lights into boxes.

The job was about as dull, repetitive and physically tiring as a job could get, and the cold of a New York winter was like nothing Gonzalez had ever experienced before: the harshness of that relentless chill penetrating deep into his bones made him long for the lazy, moist heat of Cuba.

But maybe for the first time in his life, he felt really secure, really content. He could see why so many came to America. The life he was now living was the best life he had ever had, or ever imagined he could get. Every day that he walked through the garbage strewn, graffiti-scrawled streets of East Harlem, he counted his blessings. He was deeply grateful for all that had somehow, miraculously, been delivered into his hands.

Sometimes, though, Gonzalez missed his wife, and his daughter. He missed female companionship. The love of a good woman would be the one thing that would really round out the picture and complete the bounty of his new life.

After a time living with his "mama", Ms. Acosta, Gonzales started to hang out at the hairdresser and beauty parlor owned by Acosta's daughter, Erundino Ortiz, at 1691 Boston Road, the Bronx. It is thought that he first met Lydia Feliciano either at the hairdresser, or at one of the nearby social clubs. Feliciano lived in a four-room apartment at 1010 East 178th Street in the West Farms section, several blocks from the beauty parlor and the Happy Land Club.

Lydia Feliciano, a mother of three children, was nearly ten years older than Gonzales. She was much more established and had lived in the United States for much of her life. In 1983, when the couple met, she was nearing forty, while Gonzalez had just entered his third decade. Feliciano had been living on the eighteenth floor of the Murphy Consolidation Houses in West Farms since 1971, when she had separated from her husband, Luis Torres. She lived there on a permanent basis with her daughter and two sons from her previous marriage, but the house was often packed with her many nephews and nieces. Devoutly religious, Feliciano adorned the humble, but immaculate and spacious apartment with Catholic paraphernalia including crucifixes, candles and statues of the Virgin Mary.

Despite her piety, Feliciano was also known as something of a party girl, fond of dancing and a drink. She was often found reveling late into the night to reggae and salsa at the local social clubs, especially Happy Land, where she at some point picked up a job checking coats and selling tickets for around $150 a night in wages. Feliciano loved the job, both because it brought in much needed money and because it afforded her the chance to mingle with her community. Happy Land attracted many of her country folk as well the local Hondurans. Feliciano was friendly and extroverted, one point of difference among many with the man who would become her partner for the next eight years.

Actually, from the outside, it was somewhat difficult to comprehend what had brought Julio Gonzalez and Lydia Feliciano together at all. They were markedly different in both temperament and appearance. She dressed fashionably, sometimes flamboyantly, and her natural affability drew people to her. Gonzalez was silent and timid. Slender and of average height, he didn't stand out in a crowd. He seemed to conduct himself with a kind of willful modesty. However, he did have these intense, dark eyes, that seemed to almost to stare back inward, yet see nothing. The eyes made some people uneasy. They were what the Japanese call "Panko eyes"—where an expanse of white shows below the pupils.

Feliciano, aside from being many years his senior, was short and thick set. What she lacked in conventional attractiveness, many said, she made up for by force of personality. Either way, Gonzalez wasn't in any way put off by her age or her weight. Acosta later said that from the time Gonzalez and Feliciano met, he insisted she was the only woman for him.

"He was so in love", Acosta said. And it was so sad, what happened. Feliciano broke his heart by abandoning him. Acosta never said anything blatantly negative about Feliciano, but she seemed not to care for her much. She remarked bitterly of their breakup, "she had other men".

The relationship took off exceptionally quickly. Gonzalez moved out of Acosta's apartment and into Feliciano's place in West Farms soon after the couple met, in 1983. He left his "mama" for a new hostess, with whom he was apparently smitten beyond measure.

He remained at the apartment at West Farms, apparently without incident, for the next eight years. A *New York Times* newspaper article released shortly after the night of the crime that would make Gonzales infamous referred to "a placid 8 years, angry five weeks."

In reality, nobody knows what happens behind the closed doors of a relationship.

It has almost become a cliché: in the wake of one violent catastrophe after another, another mass shooting, another murder, another rape, another assault, we hear the same tired refrain of those casually acquainted with the culprit reported in the news media: "But he was such a nice guy!" they say. "I can't believe he would even be capable of doing this," they say. "He seemed pretty average. He was friendly and polite..."

But is it that dangerous men are simply capable of blending in, chameleon-like, and seeming ordinary and nice to the outer community? A nod to the passers-by, a smile to the neighbors, home on time and relatively sober from the bar, a helping hand lent—and nobody suspects a thing. Or is it something worse? Is it that ordinary men are capable of horrendous acts of violence under the right (wrong) circumstances? And we can simply never predict with certainty how and when?

The Gonzalez case provides much food for thought in terms of these very questions.

According to neighbors, Julio Gonzalez and Lydia Feliciano lived an apparently quiet and unremarkable life together. After the event, people who knew them expressed utter disbelief about what had taken place and the charges against Gonzales.

Ms. Acosta insisted that something must have taken over Gonzalez; he couldn't have been in his right mind at the time, because that just wasn't him.

"He must have done it in a moment of fury..." she said, tears staining her eyes.

Acosta's view was shared by Antoineta, a Honduran who had known Gonzalez for some five years.

"I think something went wrong with his head. I feel really bad about it," she said. "Those were a lot of people from my country who died ... but, you know, I feel bad for him too..."

A maintenance worker at the apartment block, Patrick Pocsics, said he knew the couple well, and had never heard any arguing or fighting. Mr. Gonzales could usually be found at home and became a father figure for Feliciano's children and her numerous nephews and nieces. Gonzales was always shyly cordial, offering beer or coffee whenever Pocsics entered the apartment. "The guy was a sweetheart," Pocsics said, "He wasn't hotheaded or off the wall!"

Far from being a "hothead", Acosta described Gonzalez as having a calm, stoic demeanor. "He wasn't really one to show his emotions," she said. Her next words, meant to illustrate the point, were curiously chosen, seemingly descriptive of a person not so much emotionally even, as simply barren: "He was *never either visibly happy or unhappy*".

But Gonzalez could become wistful, she said, when he spoke of Cuba. At times, despite his love for Feliciano and the securities and comforts of his new life, he expressed a desire to return home, although he said this would be impossible because of the political situation. He missed his daughter terribly and regretted abandoning her.

Nostalgia for the homeland is hardly unusual between first generation immigrants, but when viewed alongside the other circumstances of Gonzalez's life in the period leading up to the crime, it suggests the possibility that he was more flimsily anchored in his new existence than he appeared.

He was not outgoing, and he did not have the English skills to easily make connections in the new land. He had very quickly exchanged his sponsorship situation for a live-in girlfriend. As infatuated as Gonzalez might have been with Feliciano, the move seemed to have been made impulsively, and also meant that he was abandoning an environment designed to assist him to integrate.

Although he was eligible to apply for residency under the terms of his status as a "parolee", he never actually did so. This might be significant in terms of his later actions. Although Gonzalez had relocated to America, really he was still just floating, still alien, still a stranger in a strange land. He didn't necessarily intend to stay. And he wasn't necessarily just another nice guy looking for the American Dream.

Certainly it seems that at some point prior to the breakup, Feliciano concluded this was the case—and that she didn't really know him at all. She thought she knew Gonzalez, but in truth he was a mystery to her, and what was lurking behind the quiet, placid facade may have been dark indeed. Maybe Gonzalez was a quiet guy because he was so used to being kicked around, never really wanted or welcomed anywhere, just a piece of human flotsam drifting from place to place. He never believed he really deserved anything; why speak up when there ain't nobody listening? Feliciano was the first—and last—thing that he had in life.

Feliciano had begun to suspect that Gonzalez's motives in being with her were far from pure. Two months before the fire, Feliciano accused Gonzalez of making sexual advances to her nineteen-year-old niece, Bettsabeth "Betsy" Torres, who was then living in the household. It isn't clear whether Feliciano's concerns about Gonzalez's attentions to Betsy extended to her other children and young relatives.

Some said that over time, the foundations of Feliciano and Gonzalez's connection had begun to be based more in utility than an authentic loving connection. Certainly, for eight years, Gonzalez provided assistance to Feliciano in the form of a paycheck and someone to watch the children while she was at work. But she may have begun to wonder if this was a good and safe arrangement, and whether Gonzalez's interest in her young relatives went further than simply "watching" them or acting as some kind of father figure. It is possible she had begun to regard Gonzalez as a parasite and a predator, who had hitched to her wagon for a place to live and access to her children.

Gonzalez benefited by the arrangement because he had a roof over his head, and the care and support of a loving woman. But Feliciano, slowly overtaken by feelings of suspicion and resentment, was falling out of love. And if the building blocks of security, the delicate scaffolding of togetherness —the apartment, his job, his role as a "surrogate father" to the kids—were to be taken away, perhaps there would be nothing of substance holding the relationship together.

Moreover, perhaps there would be nothing holding Gonzalez together either—and because nobody really knew or understood this relentlessly timid and silent man, it was hard to say just what he was going to do.

And that's exactly what happened.

In the final months leading up to the fire, trouble was brewing in the relationship.

Some months before the tragedy, Gonzalez lost his job at the lamp factory. Now, Gonzalez wasn't bringing in any money, and Feliciano was effectively left with a househusband who she had to support.

Gonzalez had, in their time together, set about making himself indispensable to Feliciano by taking care of her children. But there were also murmurings that, aside from any clandestine motives he might have had in so doing, that he had begun to resent this arrangement, regarding it as a slight to his machismo. His drinking pal, a man named Popo, said that Feliciano "dominated" him and got him mad.

"She went out to the club! But she made him stay home".

Feliciano's job at Happy Land was a frequent source of arguments. Gonzalez wanted her to quit and stay home. The job gave her the opportunity to meet and mingle with other men and exposed him to competitors for her affections. It also gave her a measure of financial independence and freedom that unsettled Gonzalez, particularly since it appears he was already feeling insecure about the relationship.

With Gonzalez unemployed, he was home all the time, and Feliciano did not feel comfortable leaving him at home with Betsy. The fight about Betsy Torres was the final strike against him, and Feliciano threw him out of her apartment.

Julio Gonzalez, a parolee immigrant from Cuba with tenuous connections in his new land, an uneducated loner who barely spoke English, a deceptively sanguine man possessed of an impenetrable nature and motives, was now homeless, unemployed and alone.

And he was angry about it.

* * *

About five weeks after the breakup with Feliciano, Gonzalez appeared at the beauty salon and hairdresser owned by Erundino Ortiz, Ms. Acosta's daughter. Acosta was there at the time and the two spoke at length. Gonzalez mentioned the fight that he had had with Feliciano about Betsy Torres. He framed the argument as being a product of Feliciano's jealousy: Feliciano had got all worked up and mad, she had got some spurious idea in her head that he wanted Betsy. But he insisted that he only cared for Feliciano and had no feelings at all for Betsy Torres.

"He was sad [about the fighting]", Mrs. Ortiz said. "He was really in love".

Curiously, he never mentioned to Ms. Acosta or Mrs. Ortiz that Feliciano had thrown him out of her apartment weeks earlier.

Gonzalez spent most of that Saturday in the beauty parlor. He made idle conversation with the patrons, many of whom were friends from the neighborhood, and helped Mrs. Ortiz with various odd jobs. He stayed until 6:30p.m. and left when the salon closed.

"He put his arm around me," Ms. Acosta recalled. "He said, 'You are my mamma, and I am here because of you."

Gonzalez then returned to his new, much less salubrious accommodations in the rooming house at 31 Buchanan Place, where he occupied a single room which rented for less than $100 a week. It measured about 5 by 10 feet, and was furnished with a single bed, a sink, a hotplate, a closet and a picture of Jesus against one wall. He had so far been unsuccessful in finding steady employment to replace his job at the lamp factory and was essentially surviving by begging and hustling his friends, neighbors, and anybody in the Bronx who might have a buck or few to part with.

Neighbors at the Buchanan Place apartments again described Gonzalez as quiet, but pleasant and helpful. He had offered to help them carry their groceries or do other chores. "He's neat, tidy and well-mannered," said the building's manager, Ray Davis. "He's not loud or the type of guy you would notice in a crowd."

Luis Rolan, 30, lived in the room adjoining Gonzalez's. The two would sometimes share beers of an afternoon, but according to Rolan, Gonzalez never brought up any problems with his ex-girlfriend—nor would he have expected him to. "That was just too personal. We didn't get into things like that," he said. "He's a nice guy. He didn't talk to nobody. He wasn't the kind that would do this. But you know what they say," Rolan added as an afterthought. "It's the quiet guy you have to watch for."

Given his silence and bland aura of secrecy, these witnesses never had the opportunity to learn of Gonzalez's troubled history. They never would have guessed at the mental and emotional chaos swirling behind his placid demeanor in those weeks leading up to the events of March 25, 1990.

It seemed that Gonzalez had quietly assumed a condition of utter desperation, without anyone really noticing.

He had indeed embarked on a campaign to woo Feliciano back, but without success.

Ms. Acosta recalled that on March 20, a few days after the Saturday he had come to the beauty parlor, he had turned up at the salon again, this time to meet with Feliciano. Acosta observed the two speaking, but there apparently was no argument or trouble at the time.

After a brief conversation, Feliciano left alone. Gonzalez sat silently in his chair for a while, looking utterly dejected, just staring at the floor. He then abruptly got up out of his chair and made for the door, going his own way down Boston Road.

"Lydia did not love him," Acosta said dryly. "She wanted to see other men."

This conversation between Gonzalez and Feliciano took place just a few days before the fire. Nobody knows for sure what words were exchanged at the time, but whether or not Feliciano informed Gonzalez that she was moving on with new prospects, certainly from the outside it appeared she had at a minimum rebuffed him and told him there was absolutely no hope for reconciliation.

Gonzalez went away quietly on that occasion, but on Saturday, March 25, he decided to make one last try to win her back.

That night Feliciano was working, and he sought her out at Happy Land.

Chapter 6

The social clubs of East Tremont pulsed with the sounds of *merengue*, reggae, Santana, Tito Puente and Latino disco and house, drawing enthusiastic crowds of Hispanic immigrants. Normally busy on weekends, on the night of *Puenta Carnivale*, March 25, many of the clubs were packed well beyond capacity.

Such was arguably cause for concern, as many of these social clubs operated illegally, in small, unregulated spaces. But these clandestine arrangements were also often the preference both of the patrons and the club owners. The social clubs functioned as ethnic community lynchpins, gathering places for newcomers to the United States, where recent arrivals could get to know those who were more established and access friendship, camaraderie, information and often resources.

Many of the visitors lacked proper documentation to avoid deportation and kept a low profile. Their family members and friends in the community, whether legal residents or not, often took on the same fears and attitudes of the illegal immigrants, assiduously avoiding the scrutiny of police and regulatory authorities in order to look out for and protect one another. So it was that clubs and buildings that lacked proper licenses, certifications and safety features were of little concern to those whose own documents were often not in order.

One of these clubs was Happy Land.

Those who remember Happy Land say it was a cool place, but it could be a little rough too. The young Central American male patrons often brought their machismo along to the party.

"Every weekend there were fights there," said Jose Javier, 21. Julian Guity, 18, said, "Going there was basically a form of suicide. There were shootouts, knifings… one time I was there a guy pulled out a gun next to me and shot. I ran out of there."

The major danger to those who frequented Happy Land, of course, didn't turn out to be knives or gunfire.

Passers-by would know that there was or had been at some time a nightclub inside because of the sign out the front: Happy Land in large black letters and a yellow smiling face, similar to today's smile emojis, nestled between the words "Happy" and "Land". The name came from a popular Honduran term for the United States, a shorthand description for a beckoning idyll where one could obtain a better life. In the 1980s, a wave of immigration from Honduras swelled the populations of the Bronx, and a large majority of Happy Land's patrons came from that country. Honduras is in fact the country that gave rise to the term "banana republic." The fruit was the basis of its economy, such as it was; Honduras was one of the poorest countries in the world, and its people fled from chronic social strife and political instability, wars, corruption, rampant inequality and the vulnerability of its agricultural economic base to natural disaster.

In years to come, after Happy Land became the site of one of the most deadly and shocking tragedies in New York history, the club's name became steeped in a retrospective irony. "Happy Land" was synonymous with agony, pain and misery for those who had once laughed, smiled and danced with such carefree delight.

Other than the sign, there were no hints that an active club was even in existence. It was set back from the street, and the management concealed the club's garbage amongst waste from nearby commercial retailers. It was only open on weekend nights, when building inspectors weren't around. Club patrons were forbidden from loitering outside, and the doors and sole window were blocked and soundproofed.

A "social club," under the law, was defined as a not-for-profit corporation "for the purpose of providing for members entertainment, sport, recreation and amusement of all kinds." Social clubs could implement more flexible operating hours than cabaret licensed night clubs and could charge a membership fee; however they were not permitted to sell liquor, charge admission fees or be open to the public. Happy Land was one of many clubs in the Bronx that took advantage of the status of "social club" in order to operate during hours that would support the goal of avoiding the attention of authorities, whilst also providing a meeting place with a community role; like many such clubs, however, Happy Land did indeed charge a low entry fee, sell liquor to patrons and was open to the public. It was therefore operating well outside its license parameters.

Happy Land had no occupancy certificate or public assembly permit. To secure those certifications, it would have needed to meet minimum building standards that it most certainly fell short of. There was only one functional access door, which was also the primary means of exit. On the north side of the club's frontage, there was a service entry door, but it was little used and normally blocked off by a rolling gate. On the ground floor there was a coat check area, a ticket sales booth and a bar. The primary means of access to the upstairs area was a staircase at the rear of the club. There was also a narrow, very steep staircase, almost like a ladder, at the front of the club, which was mostly used by the staff and deejays.

The upper floor, where the deejay decks and dancefloor were located, was an unapproved addition to the building that had no windows and a ceiling height of barely over seven feet. The club lacked alarms or a functional sprinkler system, apart from an outdated set of sprinklers in the upper floor.

The fact that the club would likely be a disastrous environment in the event of a fire was something that had been discussed by the club's patrons. Barbara Farrington, who lost two daughters, Debbie, 23, and Loretta, 20, said, "I told them not to go there." She told the *Daily News* that "it was supposed to be such a happy night. But everyone knew that was a deathtrap."

Maria Gale-Romero, who lost a daughter that night, had been there twice, and the crowded, windowless club worried her.

She asked her nephew Norman Omar Clark, "Where do we go if there's a fire?"

"He laughed and said c'mon, tia, we come here to dance."'

* * *

Happy Land attracted patrons from many Central American nations, but it was primarily a gathering place for the Bronx's Honduran diaspora, many of whom were Garifunas. Garifunas, sometimes known as Black Caribs, are afro-Caribbeans from the Caribbean coasts of Belize, Guatemala, Nicaragua and Honduras. The history of these people is one of displacement and dispersal, first from Africa to the island of St. Vincent, where they intermarried with local

34

populations of Arawaks and Carib Indians (Caribs)— immigrants from South America, and then to the coast of the Central American mainland where they were exiled by British troops in 1796. They are a highly distinct ethnocultural group that speak their own language, which developed due to the admixture of West African, Arawak and Carib ancestries in the homeland, and unlike most people from the Latin countries of Central America, they are Black, not Caucasian.

In 1990, Garifunas in New York comprised the largest population located outside of Central America. Even so, they were not well established, with little sense of their cohesive identity in the new city, no influence on civic processes, and no proper public space to interact. The Happy Land club served an important social function for Garifuna newcomers to New York, being one of the few places they could meet with others from their community. At Happy Land the deejays played a lot of Honduran dance music, and the bar served *Salvavida*, the national beer.

On the night of March 25, nearly a hundred people were packed into the small club. About 60 of those attendees were Hondurans, and of those Hondurans, there were around 40 Garifunas.

The patrons were excited about *Punta Carnivale*. They weren't even thinking about the safety of the building in which the celebrations were to be held.

* * *

The fact that Happy Land would be particularly busy due to the *Punta Carnivale* celebrations would not have been lost on Julio Gonzalez. Also, because he had been to the club numerous times, he knew the club's layout, that there was an absence of windows and ventilation, and that the entrance on Southern Boulevard was really the only way in or out.

Nobody will ever know quite what was going on in Gonzalez's mind when he decided to go to Happy Land that night. Was the arson attack a plan that he possibly had in reserve, already swirling in the recesses of his brain? Or was it only conceived "in a moment of fury" as Ms. Acosta thought?

What is certain is that Gonzalez was devastated and enraged over the loss of Lydia Feliciano and that for a long time he had held a huge grudge against Happy Land itself, as the place that had been the cause of so many arguments between them and the place that she was now likely meeting her new romantic "prospects."

In the months leading up to the disaster, Gonzalez had been toying with the idea of simply reporting the illegal club to the police and having it shut down.

Due to its many safety violations and its lack of fire sprinklers and exits, Happy Land had actually been ordered closed two years earlier during a crackdown in the wake of the smaller, less deadly nightclub fire at El Hoyo. Authorities scoped out Happy Land, and a Notice to Vacate was tacked on the door, but nobody followed it up. Happy Land was still operating against orders, so Gonzalez thought of letting the cops know about that, and then Feliciano would be out of a job.

For whatever reason, Gonzalez never pursued this more peaceful route to his goal. Perhaps he simply never got around to it. In the meantime, his vendetta against Happy Land continued to ferment in the dark corners of his mind.

Gonzalez had been drinking beer the night of the disaster. It is not known what time he initially arrived at Happy Land, but he was seen at the upstairs bar speaking with Lydia Feliciano at around 2:30a.m. At this time there was no eruption, and the two were observed speaking quietly, but after talking to Gonzalez for a while, Feliciano apparently told him to leave her alone.

Gonzalez slunk away with his beer, trying to disappear amongst the other club goers, trying to appear just as one of them.

But he was not at Happy Land for a party; he was alone, and he certainly wasn't enjoying himself or having a good time. He had gone there to see Feliciano. He could not leave well enough alone, and he approached her again.

This time Feliciano was more forceful in her refusal of his attentions. She told him to "get lost." And now, Gonzalez was mad as hell.

Feliciano tried to leave Gonzalez at the bar. She made to walk away, but Gonzalez grabbed her arm. A bouncer who witnessed the altercation intervened, grabbing Gonzales by the shoulder and telling him it was time to leave.

He shoved Gonzalez onwards, towards the stairs that led down to the exit on Southern Boulevard. But Gonzalez, while forcibly restrained by the bouncer, craned his head back to face Feliciano and continued shouting at her, his words an eerie warning of the tragedy to come:

"You will not work here tomorrow! You'll see! I told you and I swear it!"

The bouncer managed to eject Gonzalez from the club, but down on the street, outside the entry doors, Gonzales kept on ranting and shouting while a small crowd of patrons assembled on the street and watched on in amusement.

"I will be back!" he roared at the bouncer, at the people standing on the pavement, at anyone nearby who might listen. "I will close this place down!"

Eventually Gonzalez retreated into the night, and the bouncer thought no more of it, writing off Gonzales as just another drunk and disorderly customer who had probably gone home to sleep it off.

But Gonzalez did not go home.

Instead, he strode off towards East Tremont and Crotona Parkway, stewing in rage and resentment against Feliciano, who had rejected him—again—against the bouncer who had just thrown him out and humiliated him in public, and against Happy Land, the place that had stolen his woman.

Feliciano had cut ties with Gonzalez once and for all. And Feliciano was the only stabilizing influence in his life. Despite his efforts to woo her back, she refused to allow him to return to the comforts and security of their old shared home. Gonzalez was broke, unemployed and adrift. And now, additionally, he was furious and fueled by alcohol.

And it seems that it was at this time, if not earlier, that Gonzalez hatched his plan.

A few blocks down the street there was an Amoco gas station, at the corner of 174th Street and Southern Boulevard. Gonzalez headed there next. Along the way, he spotted an empty one-gallon Blackhawk oil container nestled in the gutter.

It was almost too perfect. His plan was obviously the right one. God was inviting him to carry it out, setting up all the circumstances for him perfectly.

The attendant at the Amoco gas station was Edward Porros, just 23 years old, a freshman at Lehman College. It was also, by happenstance, his first day on the job. Another circumstance in Gonzalez's favor.

The ordinary-looking stranger asked Porros if he could fill his cannister from the pump. He just needed a dollar's worth. That was all the cash he had right now.

Porros hesitated. Where was the man's car if he needed gas? Gonzalez told him it had broken down a few blocks away. He needed fuel to get it started again.

Porros still wasn't sure of the appropriate action to take in the situation. The request was unusual, and his training so far hadn't prepared him for it. What if the man was up to some kind of trouble?

But Gonzalez was about to get another lucky break. At that very moment, a man he vaguely knew from round the neighborhood came into the Amoco.

"Don't worry about it," the man said. "I know Julio. He's a good guy."

Feeling reassured, Porros complied with Gonzalez's request. Gonzalez put his one dollar down on the counter and out he went to the pump with his canister.

Porros returned to his duties, but for some reason, he continued to feel somewhat uneasy about the incident for the rest of his shift.

In the morning, his worst fears would come true.

Gonzalez headed back down Southern Boulevard with his dollar worth of gasoline swinging in his right hand. As he approached Happy Land, he saw that it was quiet outside the club entrance. It was now well after 3 a.m., and the patrons who had earlier been milling outside were upstairs inside the club. The music was pulsing from the deejay booth on the upper floor. Everyone was inside, drinking, dancing and having a good time. The coast was clear to enact the crime, and the victims would never escape.

But as Gonzalez approached the club, a man emerged from the shadows and eyed him suspiciously. Gonzalez turned on his heel and walked to a nearby payphone booth. There he pretended to make a phone call, until the man finally went away.

On his second try, he was successful. Nobody was watching him; nobody was there to stop the unforgivable act.

Gonzalez stepped boldly towards the club entrance. The club entry door was open but not manned. The bouncer was nowhere to be seen. Gonzalez stepped into the entryway and upended the gasoline container, emptying the violently incendiary liquid on the floor just inside the door and on the bottommost steps of the stairway leading upstairs. As it happened, some clubgoers were gathered at the top of the steps leading to the second floor. They saw Gonzalez down there, but they couldn't actually make out what he was doing.

He then reached into his pocket, withdrew his box of matches, lit two and dropped them on the ground. Then, he beat a hasty retreat to the opposite side of the street, while the flames shot up with a loud "whoosh" behind him.

There, Gonzalez stood for some time, watching the results of his work. The entryway went up immediately. Soon the fire spread to the closed service door, and the whole facade was alight.

A couple of minutes later, the fire and EMS crews had just started to arrive. Gonzalez watched as the first body was removed from the club, pretending to be another innocent bystander. Some of the firefighters and emergency workers saw Gonzalez standing there watching, but by now there was quite a crowd of gawking pedestrians in the area, and they thought he was simply another of those.

As the area outside the club was now swarming with personnel, Gonzalez left the scene and walked to East Tremont Avenue, just a block away, and waited there for the #40 bus home… as if it were any other night.

But on the bus homewards, the full reality of what he had just done began to sink in. Gonzalez believed he had killed Feliciano; he wasn't aware that she had survived. He had killed Betsy Torres, who was at the club that night. He had also probably killed other people he knew—friends and acquaintances that he had seen at the club just hours earlier.

He began to weep as the enormity of it all overwhelmed him. He already had nothing in life; everything had been taken from him, and just a short time earlier he had thought he didn't care anymore about anything. Why not burn it all down?

But once his fury was purged by this extreme act of violence, the gratification of revenge showed itself to be hollow. He still had nothing, and now he had killed a lot of people, including friends, including people he loved.

At around 4:15 a.m., Yvonne Torres, who lived down the hall from Gonzalez in the Buchanan Place roominghouse, peered out her window and saw Gonzalez enter the lobby on the ground floor. A short time later, Gonzalez knocked on the door of a neighbor, Pedro Rivera. Rivera was asleep, but his girlfriend, Carmen Melendez, heard the knocking and answered the door.

Melendez let Gonzalez into the apartment. His face damp with tears, Gonzalez collapsed at the foot of her bed. In between sobs, he finally managed to get out his words: he had killed Feliciano. He burned the club down. And as she later reported to the detectives who came to arrest Gonzalez, she didn't believe him and told him to go to bed.

Whatever sadness or remorse Gonzalez felt was apparently short-lived.

Press accounts routinely described Gonzalez as "drunk" when he committed the crime. The official police report, however, stated that on the evening of the fire Gonzalez had consumed around three beers: not a sufficient amount to make him pass out after the adrenaline kick of setting fire to a nightclub and murdering a ton of people.

Instead, despite the culprit's tears and apparent remorse, some detectives on the case put Gonzalez's ability to sleep so easily after the event down to a level of emotional callousness. It is quite possible, they said, for men in these circumstances to appear to be very sorry for their actions—but primarily, they only really only feel sorry for themselves.

Detective Moroney later remarked that he and his team were very familiar with the strange sleeping habits of violent criminals. Even after the most horrific crimes imaginable, they would fall asleep — in the back of a cop car, at the station, during booking, in cuffs... anywhere at all!

Chapter 7

Because Julio Gonzalez knew the layout of Happy Land, that it had no upstairs windows and a sole exit and that authorities indeed had already once tried to have it shut down due to its plethora of safety issues, he would have been well aware that his arson attack on the club would have caused a lot of damage and killed many people.

However, he probably would not have been aware of the scale of the tragedy that he had, in fact, unleashed. To know that, he would have had to have possessed skills and knowledge more in the realm of fire technicians and experts than laymen, such as himself.

The disaster unfolded as follows. When Gonzalez ignited the initial blaze at the foot of the steps on the club's ground floor just inside the entrance, the door from the entryway to Southern Boulevard was open. The door leading from the entryway through to the ground-floor bar was closed. The club's walls, both on the ground floor and upper level, were furnished from low-density wood paneling, while the ceilings were constructed from fiberboard tiles on the first-floor entry and bar. These materials are highly flammable, with an effect like kindling when exposed to flame. The fire rapidly spread through the internal finish in the entryway until the first escapees, alerted by the smoke, opened the door between the ground floor bar and the entryway to escape. This action opened a path for the fire into the first-floor bar area.

Additionally, the fact that this door had been left open allowed large amounts of oxygen into the building to fuel the fire. The fire then raced up the steps to the upper floor. The fact that the doors were left open was significant because the type of fire that ended up developing at Happy Land was a ventilation-controlled, as opposed to fuel-controlled, fire—meaning that it was the air available that determined the extent of the fire; and in this instance, the oxygen rapidly fueled the flames, which in turn sucked the air right out of the windowless club's second floor, where most of the patrons were located. This was why those victims that the fire personnel discovered on the second floor were, in some cases, still clutching drinks: they had died not from the fire, or even primarily smoke inhalation, but because they had suffocated.

At the time that Gonzalez lit the initial blaze just inside the entrance area, his ex-girlfriend, Lydia Feliciano was literally feet away from him. She was standing in the rear of the coat check area, just behind the entryway, on the ground floor. Ironically, given that Feliciano was arguably the principal target of Gonzalez's wrath, this gave her an advantage over others who would perish: she was the first to notice the fire.

"Fuego! Fuego!" ("Fire! Fire!") Feliciano began to scream.

Two patrons, Roberto Argueta and Orbin Nunez Galea, and a third, Elena Colon, the wife of club owner Elias Colon, were lucky to be just preparing to leave when the fire broke out. They were about to collect their coats when they heard Feliciano screaming and saw the flames engulf the entryway.

Like most people who weren't employees of the club, they thought the only way out was through the entryway—and that would mean they were going to burn alive. But Feliciano knew the little-used employee's exit on the north side of the club. She showed them the way, but when the group of four arrived, they panicked when they discovered that the door's exterior metal gate was pulled down, preventing them getting the door open. With great effort, Argueta reached between the door and the gate and managed to hoist it up sufficiently that they could push the door open wide enough to squeeze through.

Four initial survivors—Lydia Feliciano, Roberto Argueta, Orbin Nunez, and Elena Colon—rushed out into the untainted night air.

Once out on the street, Lydia Feliciano immediately hailed a taxi and went to the home of one of her adult daughters, who lived close by. She was terrified. She thought it likely that Gonzalez was still around somewhere nearby and that he was going to come after her.

So she didn't wait to speak with the police or EMS crews gathered outside the club. She never stopped at all to tell anyone where she was going or why.

* * *

On the upper floor of the club, Garifuna deejay Ruben Valladares had just put an old club favorite, *Young Lover* by the Jamaican reggae artist Coco Tea, on the turntable, and the revelers had all just sadly rushed to the dancefloor at the exact moment the fire began to spread to the second floor.

The music was loud, the crowd was dancing or otherwise distracted by their fun, and most of them had no clue at all that danger was looming.

A doorman raced up the narrow back stairs of the club. If anyone nearby was paying attention, they might have noticed that he was pursued by a light trail of smoke.

"Fire! Fire!" he shouted as he burst onto the dance floor... but the dancers hesitated, perplexed expressions stamped on their faces.

Ruben Valladares, however, had a clear view down the steep alternative staircase located at the front of the club from his elevated position behind the deejay decks. He noticed a faint glow behind the inner door, framing the darkness within a rectangle of light. He smelled the smoke, and then he knew it was true.

Valladares turned off the music and raised the house lights.

The dancers glanced around in confusion. Over the din of music and talking, most hadn't heard the warnings of the bouncer. Was there a bust going on? Had the cops arrived?

"Fire! Fire!" Valladares began screaming at the crowd.

The other of Happy Land's two doormen was on the upper floor when the fire broke out. He saw the smoke coming up from the lower floor. He knew his girlfriend was somewhere on the packed dance floor. He waded in, looking for her, shouting "Fire! Fire!"

Felipe "Phillip" Figueroa, a friend of Ruben Valladares who also spun records at the club from time to time, had been at Happy Land since about 2 a.m. At that time, when he entered the club, he recalled that he had heard an argument between Lydia Feliciano and a man he later concluded was Julio Gonzalez. About twenty minutes before the fire broke out, he happened to be on the ground floor again, near the entryway, when he heard arguing again, this time between the doorman and another man he couldn't see, outside the door.

"They were arguing," he explained. "A man said to the guy at the door, 'You're going to pay for it!'"

It was only later that Figueroa realized that these incidents, of which he had made so little at the time, were warnings of the horrific drama to come.

At 3:41a.m., nearly two hours after he arrived, Phillip was hanging out near the deejay decks on the upper floor when he heard the screams of his friend and the doorman and smelled the smoke.

"He [the doorman] was yelling in English, so I started yelling, 'Fuego! Fuego!' and suddenly everyone went crazy."

The patrons gathered on the dancefloor began to scatter and flee. But there was no apparent direction or logic to the exodus. Many were trying to locate friends and family members before they left. They didn't realize that they simply wouldn't have enough time.

"Some ran this way and that way. Some people didn't make a big deal out of it. It was just confusion," Figueroa said.

Phillip yelled to his friend Ruben. He knew it was time to get out. But Ruben had gone on a hopeless search for a friend on the dancefloor.

A group had gathered around the top of the staircase, but they were repelled by the smoke and heat coming from the lower floor. Phillip Figueroa looked down the stairs, and all he could see was smoke and the glow of fire behind the door. He decided to make a break for it anyway.

"Everyone saw me go for it," he said. "I yelled, 'Down, let's go!' "

Figueroa ran down the stairs, but he heard nobody coming behind. Briefly, he turned back and saw the frightened faces of those who just moments earlier had been drinking, dancing and having the time of their lives. They were far too scared to descend into the fire, but he knew that if they stayed where they were, they were doomed.

"There were a lot of people around those stairs, but nobody followed me. I could hear all the cries, lots of people saying, 'Mama!' I heard something explode, like a light."

Once down the stairs, Figueroa burst through the internal door but stumbled on the other side and smacked down on the floor, dislocating his wrist in the process. On the lower floor the flames were rising ominously, but he was able to cut a path through. The smoke was so thick that he couldn't see his way out; trying to locate the exit, he instead crashed into the cloakroom and was momentarily disoriented by the sight of piles of coats and jackets. Backtracking, he found himself in the corridor that connected with the service entryway exit, on the north side of the club; the same that Lydia Feliciano had escaped through.

And then, all of a sudden, he was out on the street. Miraculously, apart from the injury to his wrist, he was relatively unharmed.

Ruben Valladares was next, and last, to escape—and he wasn't as lucky as his friend.

Valladares ran down the staircase located near the deejay booth, the same one that Phillip Figueroa had taken to the lower floor. But by this time, because the service entryway door had been left open, oxygen was pouring in from the street, fueling the fire. Within the enclosed entryway area, it now roared out of control, and Valladares had no means of safe passage. His only choice was to run right through the fire, which was exactly what he did.

"I went down and the only thing I remember is that I was in the middle of the flames, in the mere entrance, and the only solution I found was to get *into* the fire and see if I could get out."

Phillip Figueroa was still standing on the street outside, having burst through the door just a moment earlier. He saw Valladares tumble out the main entry door—but at first, he didn't realize who it was.

Valladares and Figueroa had known each other for many years; both had come from Barrio Cristales in the Garifuna town of Trujillo, on the north Caribbean coast of Honduras. Figueroa had come to the United States in 1986 and, like most of his fellow Hondurans, headed straight for the Bronx. Eventually he secured a job with a furniture company in Washington Heights and earned extra cash doing deejay gigs on the side. It was through his deejay work, and Happy Land, that he came back into contact with his old friend Ruben. They renewed their friendship, bonding over music, beer and wonderful nights out at the club.

But the man that stood there trembling and moaning before Phillip on the sidewalk that morning was a stranger—an almost unrecognizable burning madman.

Ruben's face, as Figueroa later said, was "all messed up"—seriously burned, and covered in soot. But Valladares always wore a very distinctive set of gold chains around his neck. When Figueroa saw the chains, he suddenly realized it was his friend.

"He let out some screams that I'll never forget," Phillip said. "I ripped off his shirt, which was still on fire. His whole body was shaking."

In what seemed like seconds, Mr. Figueroa said, his friend was gone in an ambulance.

"I couldn't let go of his clothing," he said. "When I got to the house of his sister, to tell her, I was still holding it."

Ruben Valladares was horrifically injured in the fire at Happy Land. He received burns to over 40 percent of his body. A leather Rasta hat had saved his hair, but the hundred-dollar bill in his pocket was singed.

The ambulance took him to nearby Jacobi Hospital in the Bronx, where, once the critical period had passed and his condition was stabilized, doctors gave him only a slightly better than even chance of survival.

But he did live, as did Lydia Feliciano, Felipe Figueroa, Roberto Argueta, Orbin Nunez Galea, Elena Colon, and one of the doormen. This small handful of people were the only ones who escaped and survived the Happy Land disaster.

* * *

Now that the ground floor entryways and internal door had been opened, air poured into the building and the fire raged out of control. Once it had consumed the lower floor, there was only one place for it to go—up.

The blaze fulminated with a roaring whoosh, becoming a devouring, monstrous entity. It charged up the wooden stairs to the upper level.

Those who remained in the upstairs room were now trapped with no chance of survival. A crowd was still gathered at the top of the stairs, hopeful for escape.

As the fire erupted at the top of the stairs and burst into the space they fled in terror, but there was nowhere for them to go. There were no other exits. There were no windows. The only way out was now completely obstructed by flames.

The materials from which the club's interior had been constructed and furnished—woods and plastics—were consumed and degraded by the fire, and now a toxic plume of smoke and gases poured into the windowless room. There was no air to dilute this smoke that contained high levels of lethal compounds including cyanide, aldehydes and carbon monoxide.

These poisons can cause a severe asthma-like reaction, causing the bronchial tubes to spasm so wildly that they collapse. When there is an excess of carbon monoxide in the air, the body replaces the oxygen in red blood cells with carbon monoxide. The result can be loss of consciousness, tissue damage and death. Carbon monoxide is an especially lethal component of smoke: the gas prevents the lungs from absorbing enough oxygen to fuel the brain and heart. Carbon monoxide also blocks the activity of many of the body's vital enzymes. When the concentrations of carbon monoxide in a room reach a critical level, death usually results in about two minutes.

The crowd erupted in a futile panic as the dense smoke poured into the upper level.

Some club patrons fell to the floor, desperate for a gasp of unspoiled air. But it was not long before the smoke and gas filled every inch and cranny of the room.

The victims now began to succumb to unconsciousness, staggering and tumbling into tables, walls and each other. There was no hope for survival, only for a few final seconds of love and comfort before the inevitable end—and so the people, many of whom were from the same families and tight-knit friendship groups, simply clung to each other where they sat or lay.

Within the space of three minutes, everyone was dead. They didn't die from the fire. There were no burn marks on their skin, and their clothes remained clean and sharp. They had died purely from the inhalation of smoke and gases, and deprivation of oxygen.

Dr. Roger Yurta of the Medical Examiner's office later said: "If you consider together carbon monoxide poisoning, oxygen deprivation and the effects of toxic substances in the smoke, death could in some cases be almost immediate, within a matter of seconds."

* * *

Frank J. Nastro, assistant chief of department for the City of New York Fire Department, was a veteran of the FDNY, having spent some 33 years in its employ. In 1990 he was in charge of special operations command, a role that saw him overseeing responsibility for coordinating the response to critical incidents such as Happy Land.

The initial notification to his office was for two 10.45 Code 1s at a fire in the Bronx. This meant that at first, all the FDNY knew was that there were two seriously injured, and two fatalities (10.45 is the signal for seriously injured; Code 1 notifies a fatality).

By the time Nastro had dressed in preparation to leave the command center, a second notification came through: the count had now suddenly risen to 24.

Stunned, Nastro rapidly marshalled his team, and they barreled out of the command center. As they hurried up the East River Drive, a third update came through: the aide from Division 7 got on the radio and transmitted a 10.45 count of *fifty* to the dispatcher. The dispatcher responded, asking what code they were. "Code 1," came the answer. Fifty fatalities.

"When I heard that," Nastro later said, "I nearly fell out of the car."

The fire department had received the alarm just a minute after Gonzalez lit the initial blaze. They arrived in under three minutes.

Dennis Devlin was one of the first firefighters on the scene.

"There was someone in the street talking to us, telling us there was loads of people inside, trapped."

But it was eerily quiet. If there were people trapped inside, why was it so silent?

"There were no screams. There was no sound at all."

Pulling up to the curb, the men spotted Ruben Valladares on the pavement. EMS Lieutenant Roy David later described his horror at seeing the deejay staggering out onto the street, his clothes sticking to his burnt skin.

"He walked towards me. He couldn't talk. All we could do was treat him."

Phillip Figueroa was there, too, and unlike Ruben, mostly unscathed. This would arouse the suspicions of the detectives shortly to arrive at the scene. How had he survived without any burns; how had he come through the burning entrance without getting hurt?

Unless, of course, he himself was the perpetrator. The cops detained Figueroa as both a key witness and a suspect—until Gonzalez's confession later placed him in the clear. His testimony would be important in piecing the case together, and at the eventual trial.

* * *

Frank Nastro, Commissioner Carlos Rivera, Chief of Operations William Feehan and fourth-alarm Chief Anthony DeVita were the first to enter the structure.

They noted some burns on the bodies of the initial 19 victims retrieved from the lower floor. These people had died in the ground floor bar or on the staircase in a fruitless rush for the exit. The officers immediately concluded that they had died of smoke inhalation, as their burns were not extensive.

The bodies were laid out on the sidewalk and covered with white sheeting. Morning was now approaching, and soon a mass of curious, horrified passers-by gathered around the makeshift morgue on Southern Boulevard. The press corps descended, and the first photographs, showing the burnt exterior of Happy Land and the grim specter of sheathed corpses laid out side by side right there on the pavement, were taken for the papers.

The time taken for the 150 firefighters who were dispatched to the site to extinguish the blaze was blessedly brief: less than five minutes. The fire had not burned through to the second floor.

Once that task was accomplished, the firefighters ascended the rear stairs, picking their way over bodies. The stairs were lined with the bodies of those who had been trying to get to the lower floor to escape but simply didn't have enough time. On the landing above there were many more, and the second-floor doorway was choked with victims—they had literally died while running for their lives.

The FDNY officers knew that the scene on the upper floor would be grim; they had felt the bodies under their feet. But the room had to be ventilated of smoke before they could fully appreciate what they were dealing with.

"The smoke was so heavy you couldn't see anything," Firefighter Frank Curtin later explained. "We were actually stepping on bodies downstairs before we realized we had people in there."

Chief Kenneth Cerreta was a deputy in Division 7 of the WNYF. He involuntarily gasped as the smoke lifted and the small space, littered with the bodies of young people who appeared to be sleeping, revealed itself in its full horror.

"As the magnitude of the tragedy was uncovered, [it was] so enormous, it was hard to fathom. It was the worst thing I'd ever seen ... just the worst."

The victims lay in tangled heaps on the floor, grasping each other, or clawing at their own throats. The only indication of fire on these bodies was some slightly darkened skin and clothing where soot fragments had settled.

Most of the victims upstairs were trapped among a group of tables near the dance floor. Some were found cowering behind the bar. The victims were "huddled together" and "looked mostly in their thirties or younger," Roy David said. Firefighter Dan DeFranco added: "Many of the bodies that were upstairs were still seated upright at tables."

The bodies in some places were piled one on top of the other.

"It was just devastating," Dennis Devlin said. "As soon as you would pick a body up, there would be two bodies under it. Some of them fused together from the heat."

Nastro and his men noted that there was a simple, older-style branch sprinkler system on the upper floor. Four sprinklers had activated, but even if that had come in time, it had no effect on the fire, which was rising from the floor below. Ironically, there was no sprinkler system on the lower floor, where it was needed.

Because there was no fire upstairs, Nastro dismissed a large proportion of his team from the scene and told them to leave the building.

"There were no operational duties to be performed at this time, and it would have been unfair to subject them to such a stressful scene needlessly."

Several firefighters were already displaying intense emotional reactions and signs of trauma. If they hadn't thrown up from the shock of what they had seen, they were reduced to wandering around in a daze, unable to speak.

The FDNY, recognizing the enormity of the stress their men had been subjected to, ordered critical incident stress debriefing immediately. Chaplains, medical officers and counseling units responded to the scene. Many of these seasoned firefighters were so deeply affected by what they saw that they required counselling and leave of absence before they could return to work.

A counselor described a group of people who, to him, resembled war veterans with shellshock. "Their eyes had the hollow and distant look of men who could not believe what had occurred."

A certain description of the scene came up again and again. It wasn't just a fire, the men said. It was a *gas chamber.*

For some, it was the first time they had seen the worst a fire could do, and for others, it was the first time they had seen the worst possible outcome of a fire of this type, where the real risk wasn't flames or even smoke, but a combination of lethal gasses and lack of oxygen.

The longer-range consequences of Happy Land, not only for the FDNY but police officers and the EMS, was that they would lose their confidence in a once firmly held conviction that if they got to an emergency scene in time, and did their job to the best of their ability, the result would be successful, no matter the balance of circumstances.

"Happy Land broke our self-belief, in a way," one firefighter said. "Firemen are the hero-type of guys. We want to help, we want to save lives, we want to bring back something positive from a situation of tragedy. This time, we couldn't do anything. We couldn't help anyone. It all just happened so fast. They had all died before we got there... and believe me, we didn't waste any time at all getting to that scene."

Chapter 8

Outside Happy Land, TV crews had descended to broadcast the vigil of friends and relatives waiting for word on their loved ones, recordings in which those left behind vented feelings of outrage, frustration and powerlessness.

"I hope he isn't in there," one woman said, "but I heard he was going to the club last night."

Others, such as a woman named Lynella Boden, seemed to have already given up hope—a reasonable stance given so few had apparently survived.

"There's no way to describe what I'm feeling right now. There are no words..."

Bodies continued to pile up on the pavement, covered in shrouds. The process of removal was slow, adding to everyone's unease. There were insufficient body bags to remove all the victims, so the New York Port Authority, which responds to aircraft incidents, provided the FDNY with an additional sixty body bags.

The area where the shrouded bodies had been laid on the pavement, including the access route for bodies being removed into trucks to be taken away for identification, had been cordoned off, but the crowd grew increasingly restless in their need to know the whereabouts of loved ones. Soon some were attempting to crash through the barricade. The WABC coverage of the incident showed a near hysterical man being manhandled away from the site by detectives. "My brother is in there!" the man wailed in anguish.

The situation was becoming unmanageable, and soon authorities set up the new command center away from the site, at nearby Public School 57, so that firefighters, police and EMS staff could complete their work uninterrupted. Those gathered were advised to go to the school and wait there for information.

Over at the 48th precinct, police began the slow and tedious process of sorting through the clothing and personal belongings of the victims. Once identified, the bodies were tagged and their faces photographed. The photographs would be sent to the school to permit identification by relatives.

* * *

As the morning wore on, the grotesque revelations about the scene inside Happy Land continued.

Firefighters and EMS personnel had seen things that shocked them to their very core. One after another, the men appeared on newscasts, ashen-faced and visibly shaken, struggling to find words for what they had witnessed.

"This is the worst thing I have ever seen in my career," EMS specialist Christopher McCarthy said. "It hurt my stomach. It was sickening. Most of the bodies were in dance clothes. They were out to have fun... I saw wall-to-wall bodies—an indication of mass confusion and panic."

A Red Cross worker told the press that some of those trapped had punched a hole through a wall to the adjoining union hall in their desperation to escape. The victims had clearly been in a state of pure and desperate terror, frantic to survive. But, as EMS Executive Director Thomas Doyle said, "There was no way out. They never had a chance."

The FDNY revealed the sad finding that there had only been a single fire extinguisher in the building. It was found clutched in the hands of the club manager as he lay dead on the stairs, right where he dropped. "He never had a chance to pull the pin," Nastro later remarked.

The New York City Medical Examiner were still faced with the task of determining an exact cause and time of death for each of the 87 victims. But what was clear at this early stage was that these people, particularly those on the upper floor, had died at an unbelievable speed not often seen in fatal fires.

The principal theory for why this had occurred, as outlined above, was oxygen deprivation and toxins in the smoke. EMS representatives, however, at this time floated an alternative theory. Some of them thought that those things alone could not account for "death in seconds, not minutes."

They suspected that the fire in the enclosed building had perhaps gotten so hot so quickly that it had released superheated gasses, with temperatures in the order of 1600 to 1800 degrees Fahrenheit. This phenomenon is the one most feared by firefighters, called a flashover. One possible consequence of a flashover if there are humans in the space is that the superheated gasses could sear their airways before the fire even got to them. This would prevent them taking another breath and kill them instantly—even as they clutched a drink or sat at a table.

Dr. Charles Hirth, the Chief Medical Examiner, disputed the flashover theory. "If that had happened, you'd expect to see blistering on the walls of the club, and that was not observed," he said. "But there's still a lot of speculation flying about."

Even if a flashover had not occurred, there was an indication that the temperature in the upper room had gotten extremely hot. This was shown by the fused condition of some bodies, which demonstrated that the heat was in the order of a range where fat begins to melt.

Whatever the explanation, this was a fire with consequences the likes of which few even thought possible. It seemed crazy that it could even happen. And now that the full dimensions of the tragedy had become clear to all, it was time to ask the hard questions.

For the simple fact that an arson attack had taken place was only one part of the explanation for the extent and severity of the disaster. The other was Happy Land itself, its complete inadequacy as a nightclub venue and the fact that it was operating at all.

In the months and years to come, those still living who were affected by the catastrophe, including the friends and families of the victims, would point the finger of blame not only at Julio Gonzalez, but negligence and incompetence on the part of authorities that bordered on callousness.

The top of that list was, of course, the mayor. David Dinkins arrived at the scene, flanked by detectives, firefighters and EMS representatives, on the morning of March 25 to field questions from the press and provide reassurances to the public regarding the identification of victims, provision of assistance to relatives and his office's role in preventing any repeat of the disaster.

Dinkins, the first (and to date, the only) black American to hold the post of mayor of New York, had only been in office for a few months when the Happy Land tragedy occurred. He was relatively untried in the role, but Dinkins had pledged on ascension to be a force promoting racial healing in the city, which he famously described as "a gorgeous mosaic" of diversity, more than just a "melting pot." People in the community fully expected him to handle the disaster in a way consistent with that promise; in other words, some were hopeful that the city's response might spearhead positive efforts towards recognition and inclusiveness as far as those most affected were concerned.

Many would ultimately be disappointed. As author Wilbur C. Rich observed, " 'healing' was the central theme of the Dinkins campaign. Later racial incidents proved how difficult being a healer could be."

The Happy Land tragedy occurred against the backdrop of broader changes in American society during the late 1980s and 1990s which, retrospectively, appear somewhat of a historical "blip" on the longer timeline. The era was characterized by ebullience at the end of the Cold War and a conviction that the United States had a mission to spread democracy to the world. Multiculturalism, which has now largely fallen out of favor in the United States, was also in ascendance as an influential political ideal. Unfortunately, the zeal for democracy was used to justify wars and the propping up of puppet regimes in Central American countries that drove more and more immigrants from these countries to the United States, and into New York. Tensions rose with the explosion of immigration. And some commentators observed that, however well intentioned, the political embrace of multiculturalism in New York provided a convenient excuse for neglect of certain boroughs with high ethnic and black populations, such as the Bronx—the idea being that "self-determination" for these communities should mean letting them "do their own thing". In other words, an ideology became a convenient veil for an attitude of slackness and indifference on the part of authorities where these communities were concerned, and a way to slice costs. In the Bronx during this time, for example, many reported cases of child abuse and neglect went unmonitored and overlooked. Below you will see how such public attitudes, in interaction with an immigrant community, played out in the Happy Land disaster.

Despite Dinkins' proclamations about fairness and diversity, his reputation was already tarnished by perceptions that he was an "out of touch" wealthy black man whose refined tastes and preoccupation with his image was outside of his background and would end up being costly to taxpayers. His first few weeks in office were marred by a media scandal about an expensive Cherrywood headboard he had ordered for his wife, while fifteen thousand layoffs and a cutback on city services was being proposed.

On the day, Dinkins donned a white firefighter's hat and coat in solidarity with the men who were at that moment still removing bodies from the building. Certain segments of the press received the move cynically. "It was perhaps his first public appearance as Mayor in anything other than a tie or tennis clothes, and he seemed self-conscious," mocked one reporter. The insinuation was that he was preoccupied with his appearance even at a scene of tragedy.

In truth, Dinkins appeared remarkably compassionate and dignified by the standards of today's politicians. He offered none of the standard-issue "hopes and prayers" such as we are familiar with today after terrible public tragedies and outbreaks of violence.

And nobody could dispute the authentic distress written on the man's face after being given a tour of the interior of the club and the makeshift morgue in the adjoining building. He emerged pale and shaky, a light sheen of perspiration covering his face.

He had witnessed firsthand the same terrible sights that had so shocked the firefighters and EMS staff: rows of people that appeared to be sleeping, who had suffocated to death in a prison where the only means of egress was on fire. So shocking was it to him that he had returned to take a second look, even though he was under no obligation to go in there at all.

"I started to leave, then I turned back, I said I wanted to go back and look again. Because I just wanted it really etched in my mind what was there," he told reporters. "This was the most horrendous circumstance I've ever viewed. To go through that building, go upstairs and look at all the bodies lined up there, very graphically brought home to me the situation. I'm glad that I went, in the sense that had I not seen it, I don't think I would have appreciated it." He added during an address later that day: "Even the people in the Triangle Shirtwaist fire had the option to jump out the windows. In this case, there was no way out of there, except for the front door."

The Triangle Shirtwaist incident was a fire at a garment factory in Greenwich Village in which 146 workers were killed, and also the deadliest industrial disaster in New York history. Comparisons were naturally drawn between Happy Land and the Triangle Shirtwaist fire because, bizarrely, they had occurred on the same date, March 25—it was just that the latter had happened nearly eighty years earlier, in 1911. Also, as Dinkins noted, the victims were largely immigrants.

Despite the fact that Dinkins was transparently distressed by the tragedy, he was, after all, the mayor. Whatever his personal feelings were, the next phase of the response would reveal him to be another administrator hamstrung by the laborious politics and bureaucratic machinery of New York City. Having battled through a somber and painful morning, he very quickly moved on to the questions and reputational threats this event posed for his office.

Predictably, just as his predecessors had done many times throughout the city's history, Dinkins declared a new and unprecedentedly harsh crackdown on New York's illegal nightlife. A new "war" on illegal clubs. He vowed to shut every last one down and to ensure rigorous checks of those still permitted to operate to ensure they met safety standards.

It was estimated at the time that there were some 700 social clubs like Happy Land, mainly in Brooklyn and the Bronx. A Social Club Task Force would be ordered to investigate 227 known active clubs and an additional 1,250 believed to be inactive in New York city.

Indeed, an inspection sweep was commenced on the Sunday night following the disaster. More than 100 police officers, firefighters and building inspectors visited 179 illegal social clubs, but 165 were not open, probably because few customarily operated then. The special teams apparently ordered the remaining 14 clubs closed, and eight others were reported to authorities by callers dialing 911.

The situation grew more uncomfortable for Dinkins when the public learned that Happy Land had still been allowed to operate for 16 months after it was ordered closed for fire code violations, and that special inspection units—created after six people died in the 1988 fire at El Hoyo—had become largely inactive.

Following that fire, there was a crackdown on illegal social clubs during which a task force closed down 15 clubs, charging many violations. Happy Land was one of the clubs that had been given a notice to vacate. But all that had happened was that there was a letter tacked to the door. The club hadn't been open at the time the inspectors came through—and they never went back to check whether it ever actually closed down.

Dinkins as much as admitted that the authorities had dropped the ball. The tragedy need not have happened had they diligently carried out the duties they were entrusted with.

"We are haunted by the realization that it is a nightmare that could have been prevented... in retrospect, there's a lot of things we see now that might have been done differently."

City representatives tried to defend their lack of consistent action to date, pointing to the logistical impossibilities of fully policing the clubs and eradicating the problem with the available resources and apathetic community attitudes. Norman Steisel, first deputy mayor, told reporters that keeping track of the activities of so many clubs had historically been nightmarishly difficult.

"Even if you pull the license, give orders for them to stop operating, they just go back into business, and regrettably our inspectors are not out at night... or if you look at this place, even if you drive by it and you know it's there, you can't imagine it's a club. We need the community's help to tell us or alert us about these kinds of problems... It's not possible to do it through routine inspections I would think."

Almost in the same breath as the city promised they would close down illegal clubs, they seemed to be admitting defeat. After all, the immigrants who visited the social clubs, many of them illegals or those wanting to protect illegals, could surely not be expected to "alert the authorities."

On several occasions Dinkins came back to a particular point, that a portion of the responsibility rested with immigrant populations to stay away from illegal social clubs. The core problem, as he saw it, wasn't simply that illegal clubs were operating, but that people weren't fully aware of—or simply didn't care about—the dangers.

"It is an understatement to say this is a tragedy of immense proportions. Anybody operating such a place or thinking about going to such a place should take a look inside... part of what we need the media to assist us in doing, is to spread the tale of these gruesome circumstances, so that the general public will know that these are not safe places to which to go. And believe me if anyone could view it and witness it they would not wish to go. I don't care how good the music, how fine the company, or how great the camaraderie, they would not want to be there."

For some, a big crackdown on the illegal clubs was a matter of too little, too late. For others the mayor's sudden dedication to eradicating unlicensed social clubs overlooked a deeper and more important question: why they were operating in the first place. The social clubs fulfilled a need for migrant communities and Central and South American diaspora in New York. Cracking down on them was necessary to protect lives, but it also felt like a punishment for these communities when there was nothing to replace them with.

For it was patently absurd to expect that the kinds of folks who visited Happy Land would be keen to go to one of the larger established New York nightclubs. Clubs that had the resources to gain the appropriate permits and licenses, and to inhabit buildings that met with relevant safety and building standards, also tended to clubs with high entry fees and expensive drink prices. They were also mainstream clubs with popular top-40 music and a clientele drawn from wealthier groups and tourists. They just weren't community clubs. Such well-regulated and commercial venues were precisely the ones that immigrants wanted to stay away from, if they knew what was good for them.

The social club patrons did not have alternative and affordable public gathering places where they, as recent immigrants, could be comfortable or find welcome. This was shown by developments down the track, after Happy Land was destroyed: Garifunas started to gather at Bill Rainey Park, the Crotona Park strip located on Southern Boulevard popularly known as the "Trujillanos' Park" among the Garifunas. This informal meeting place attracted negative attention from the neighbors who lived in the area, who complained of noise, trash, and unsanitary conditions. "Garifunas are drunk, yell and curse at kids, there are too many kids running around, leave both the park and street dirty," a local said to reporters, concluding that "Garifunas are a bad influence" on the community. In other words, the destruction of social clubs, without the provision of alternatives, would lead to the situation that Garifunas feared: exposure to racism and negative judgment.

One Garifuna local appeared on the news offering a direct commentary on the city's handling of the tragedy and the tensions that were being revealed in its wake: "They don't want us here. That's what this is really all about."

In the first ten days after the Happy Land fire, Dinkins's Social Club Taskforce shut down some 36 social clubs found to be in violation of fire safety laws. The crackdown was unprecedented in its speed and vigor, and predictably, some in the community felt that it opened up a vacuum of appropriate social gathering spaces—and that some clubs had been unfairly targeted, such as those that operated in proper accordance with their social club licensing, unlike Happy Land.

Hispanic communities in the Lower East Side and Harlem began to petition the Dinkins administration to not close down "social clubs that served vital cultural, economic, and educational needs." Such clubs, run by small neighborhood groups, did not have the financial resources to upgrade to comply with the building codes and other relevant requirements.

Immigrant voices in the Bronx began to take Dinkins to task: why not earmark some of the money spent on police and building inspectors to create safe social spaces for immigrants in New York? Why not—instead of closing the social clubs down—provide assistance to bring them up to standard?

* * *

Meantime, the murky and complex history of the unserviceable building that housed Happy Land was emerging.

The building was constructed in 1921, before laws came in requiring new buildings to have a certificate of occupancy in 1938. It was a one-story structure in 1961 but showed up on city records as a two-story building in 1971. The upper floor of Happy Land was an illegal addition made some time between those two dates. There was no permit or approval given by the relevant agencies for the addition, and as such, it never even had the opportunity to comply with minimum standards. This resulted in an upper structure with no windows and a ceiling barely over seven feet from the floor, both major contributing factors to the lethality of gas and oxygen starvation in the 22-by-58-foot space.

In 1981, the then-owner was issued with several violation orders following an inspection during which it was determined that the building lacked nearly every permit and license required, and that it was surreptitiously operating as a nightclub on the upper floor. Consumer Affairs and the Buildings Department were alerted of the illegal operation of the club and bar and the absence of required permits, and subsequently, FDNY performed annual inspections. "No access" entries were recorded on the building's file for 1981 and 1982. FDNY, police and Building Department inspectors visited the building on numerous subsequent occasions, but there was a lack of coordination between the agencies. This meant that the appropriate follow up simply never happened.

Prior to the Happy Land fire, the emphasis of agency surveillance of social clubs was on the associated nuisance noise, drugs, violence and street crime. Advice of violations other than those that came under the jurisdiction of the police would sometimes go missing, be overlooked, and consequently not be acted upon. One reason for this was that police teams operated on weekends and in the evenings, and the Fire Prevention Bureau and the Buildings Department operated during business hours.

Along with a strip of stores on Southern Boulevard and East Tremont Avenue, the building was purchased on June 5, 1985, for $885,000 by a corporation controlled by Alex DiLorenzo III, a realty developer whose father was once one of the largest property owners in New York. Mr. DiLorenzo's father, Alex

DiLorenzo II, along with partner Sol Goldman, purchased hundreds of properties in the 1960s and 1970s, including the Chrysler building. Happy Land and similar clubs across the Bronx were total dumps, but the buildings were owned by wealthy New York elites.

Alex DiLorenzo was still listed as owner of the building at the time of the fire, but he had by then leased the building to Jay Weiss and Morris Jaffe of Little Peach Realty Inc., who in turn acted as managing agents.

A curious fact about Weiss was that he was, at the time, the husband of Hollywood actress Kathleen Turner. Turner was later reported as remarking with reference to the disaster, "the fire was unfortunate, but could have happened at a McDonalds"—a statement that rankled many in the Bronx, given that it was not only demonstrably untrue, but reflected a shockingly distanced and out-of-touch mindset they felt was typical of white elites when discussing the adverse experiences that affected their communities.

In 1987, Weiss and Jaffe's company leased the building space for seven years to the club owner, Elias Colon. Some time before the tragedy, Colon had the place remodeled with scant regard to safety features. The revamp was an opportunity to address the lack of windows, exits, sprinklers and alarms, but Colon's main concern was that the club remain inconspicuous and hidden: as such it was left with only the two exits at the front, a third at the back which had a gate that had been soldered shut, and one window on the ground floor that was barred and blocked from the inside with a slab of cinderblock. Colon had also ignored repeated warnings about licensing and safety violations.

In 1988 the FDNY inspected the building and, finding no certificate of occupancy, implemented surveillance to determine if an illegal occupancy was in effect. The FDNY suspected such and referred the matter to the Buildings Department who conducted an inspection in November 1988, following the El Hoyo club fire. A long list of violations were cited, including no place of public assembly (PPA) permit, lack of egress, no exit signs, operating as a social club without a permit, lack of emergency lighting, no interior fire alarm, and inadequate sprinklers. Violation orders were issued, and subsequently FDNY instituted a new round of surveillance during which the Notice to Vacate was issued.

If there was ever a time when disaster might have been averted, it was during the crackdown following the El Hoyo fire in 1988. But the lack of coordination between agencies continued to undermine any efforts to close Happy Land down or bring it into compliance with standards and regulations.

When fire and building inspectors checked on the building, it was daylight business hours, and there was no evidence the club was in operation. Police inspectors who were on their beats at night were less concerned with the fire and safety hazards presented by the club and were instead preoccupied with drugs, noise and street crime. Cops on the street did not pass word of the club's activities up the chain of command. And the two authorities did not communicate with each other.

After the fire, Thomas P. Mulligan, lieutenant in the Operations Division of the Fire Department of New York remarked, "In all the years I was in the Tower Ladder 58, near the Happy Land club, I can't recall ever having seen this club operating or seeing any indication that this building was occupied. The Happy Land Social Club was open only on weekends, did not allow patrons to loiter in front of the building, put its garbage out on East Tremont Avenue (with the commercial occupancies' garbage), and had all openings blocked and soundproofed."

* * *

As the revelations about the bureaucratic mismanagement behind the building's history continued, public anger swelled.

Happy Land, and many clubs like it—dangerous fire traps—had kept operating despite multiple opportunities for intervention and correction by the authorities.

The most critical voices charged that it was just another example of the implicitly racist indifference with which the communities of the Bronx were regarded by elites and authorities. In reality, they claimed, nobody had cared about these people until the press around the fire brought negative attention on the administration. And actually, they still didn't.

And then there were the building's owners and leaseholders. The building, inadequate and dangerous as it was, was owned by one of the richest men in New York! And yet he neither apparently knew nor cared about the conditions inside.

City officials stated in the wake of the fire that criminal negligence or even manslaughter charges could be brought against the building owners or its leaseholders.

However, it turned out that DiLorenzo, Weiss and Jaffe were in no way responsible under the agreement that was in effect for the maintenance or daily operation of the building, being the classic "absentee landlords." Similar agreements covered other substandard buildings all over New York. The landlords collected the money, but the law seemed to largely shield them from responsibility.

Furthermore, they had tried to close the club and evict its operator. Roger Boyle, a lawyer representing Little Peach, issued a statement on March 26 that Little Peach Realty Inc. had been actively pressing eviction proceedings against Elias Colon and that a trial had been scheduled to start on March 28. "Mr. Jaffe and Mr. Weiss are horrified at the events of this weekend and lament the loss of life which ensued from such events." The ironies inherent in this revelation were rich. Gonzalez's attack on the club was poor timing indeed. Had his breakup with Lydia Feliciano occurred down the track, for instance, it is possible that by that time the club would not have been operating.

The general feeling on the part of authorities was that the weight of criminal responsibility for the event, aside from Gonzalez himself, rested with Elias Colon. But Mr. Colon had died in the fire. He could not be brought to account. Further, even if Colon had survived, the eviction trial would have been moot: as it was, immediately following the fire, the building was condemned and ordered to be demolished.

Chapter 9

On the afternoon of March 25, once hauled into the precinct, Gonzalez issued a comprehensive and unambiguous voluntary confession of his crime. He cried intermittently as he described in detail the events of the previous evening: how he had gone to the club to talk to Feliciano, and how he had become consumed by rage when turned away by her and further stung by humiliation when ejected by the bouncer. How he had walked to the gas station and talked the attendant into giving him gasoline in exchange for his last dollar. How he had dumped the gasoline at the entrance and set it alight, knowing full well it was the only way in or out. How he had watched the club go up in flames, until the authorities arrived and his presence became too risky. And how he had cried on the bus home as he came to a full appreciation of what he had done.

The officers had now had some time to form a more complete picture of the man at the center of the case. And what they saw was a broken individual who had lost all interest in what fate befell him. The guy responsible for so much carnage did not appear frightening in the least as he sat in his chair. He was small, pathetic, and utterly pitiful.

"Why did you do it?" they asked him.

Gonzalez said it was for revenge. He was angry at Lydia Feliciano for leaving him, and once it had become clear she wouldn't take him back, he decided to finish her.

As plain-spoken as he had proven so far, and despite police spokesman Lt. Raymond O'Donnell's later characterization of him as "remorseful," Gonzalez didn't quite accept full responsibility. He instead resorted to that well-worn refrain of so many men convicted of abusive and violent actions: something took over him; he just "lost it."

"I don't know," he told the detectives. "It looks like something bad got into me, it looks like the devil got into me!"

That did not tally with the serious evidence of premeditation in the case: the time taken for Gonzalez to walk to the gas station, fill his canister with gasoline, and head back to the club was more than enough to change his mind about what he planned to do and fully contemplate the possible consequences. And Gonzalez had observably behaved in a calculating fashion. He had lied to Edward Porros, convincing him he needed the gas for his broken-down car—but that car did not exist.

Either way, Gonzalez had owned up to setting fire to the club. And with that, nothing remained for the officers to do than dispatch the culprit to court for the dispensation of justice.

Gonzalez was arraigned at Bronx Criminal Court at 2 a.m. on March 20, 1990. The charges were astonishing in the regard that, as prosecutor and Assistant District Attorney Eric Warner stated, theoretically they could have yielded a sentence of 2,000 years should each individual count have been added into one continuously served term. In practice, of course, the law doesn't work that way.

The charges were: 174 counts of murder, where two counts were extracted for each victim on the basis of both felony murder and "depraved indifference" to human life; one count of arson; one count of second-degree arson, in recognition of the fact that the attack resulted in damage to the property in addition to harm and death of the occupants; one count of attempted murder, on the basis that Lydia Feliciano had been an intended victim who only happened to be spared by her own efforts to escape, and that Gonzalez had acted with the intent to kill her; and one count of assault (against the bouncer).

Gonzalez, dressed in a three-piece dark blue suit and a yellow shirt, kept his eyes fixed to the floor and remained silent for most of the ten-minute session. The defendant's demeanor was largely unreadable. He seemed devoid of thought or emotion. If there was any expression at all, it was not much more than a kind of sullen dejectedness.

After two hours of deliberation, the grand jury came back with their answer: they voted to indict Mr. Gonzalez on all listed charges.

But Gonzalez then did something unexpected and outrageous.

He entered his plea as "not guilty."

At this time, his defense attorney, Richard Berne, did not make known the reasoning behind the plea, which raised many eyebrows and salted the wounds of the Bronx community given that it was clear and obvious to all that Gonzalez had willfully started the fire that took 87 lives.

As Bronx District Attorney Robert Johnson said in a news conference held the following Monday, Gonzalez had known in advance that by starting a fire in that particular building he was condemning the occupants to death; he had "forced the occupants of the club to choose between remaining inside or breaching a wall of flame at the doorways."

And yet, even after his confession, he was claiming innocence. The direction the defense was taking made people angry and uneasy.

His plea notwithstanding, naturally bail was to be denied. But there was one bright spot for Gonzalez—he would be held at a psychiatric ward at Bellevue Hospital until trial, instead of in prison. Gonzalez had cried intermittently throughout his confession and had threatened suicide. Judge Alexander Hunter accepted that there was a real risk the perpetrator might follow through and try to take his own life. It was the court's duty to ensure he received proper evaluation—but the decision also foreshadowed the ultimate direction Gonzalez's defense would take, confirming the worst fears of the victims' relatives.

* * *

Over the following days, news and television reports documented an incredible outpouring of grief on the streets of the Bronx.

Once the process of identifying all 87 victims and notifying the relatives had been completed, the true extent and nature of the tragedy became painfully clear. In particular, the fire constituted a catastrophic trauma and loss for Honduran and Garifuna peoples, both in New York and across the Caribbean Sea.

Of the victims, 59 were recent arrivals from Honduras. Of those, some seventy percent were of Garifuna descent. Back in Honduras, the papers were filled with reports on the fire for days on end, and there, the hometowns of those who were killed were thrown deep into mourning.

Any disaster with such a horrific loss of life touches the lives of friends and families of those killed in ways we cannot fathom. With the Happy Land tragedy, there was an additional dimension to the grief in that the club had been a central locus point for the Honduran and Garifuna community in New York; this meant that there was barely a Honduran alive in New York who was not affected. Many victims were related. The victims knew each other, and the families of the victims knew each other. And worst of all, many families had lost several members in one swoop due to the fire. Overnight, more than 90 children became orphans, and over forty parents lost their children, often more than one. In the worst case, one family lost twelve members.

Maria Gale-Romero had been to Happy Land twice before but was not there the night of the fire, as she had another party to attend. Sadly, her nieces and nephews decided to attend the *Punta* celebrations at Happy Land. At around 4 a.m., Gale-Romero heard that something bad had happened at the club.

"My heart fell, my legs shook."

She rushed over to 1959 Southern Boulevard, but amongst the anguished crowd gathered outside, there was no sign of her loved ones. They were all trapped inside, and they were already dead: two nieces, Alba Escoto Romero, 18, and Wendy Manaiza, 19; and three nephews, Clark, 17, Luis Manaiza, 22, and Query Romero, 33.

The communal nature of Happy Land also meant that it was not just entire families but clubs and institutions that were affected.

Five of the victims were teenagers attending Roosevelt High School in nearby Fordham. A memorial service was held at the school in April 1990. The Honduran community's soccer team also lost ten members, almost all young people between the ages of 18 and 23, because Happy Land had been its unofficial headquarters. "Sadly, it was a young people's club mostly," coach Miguel A. Reyes later said.

Several of the victims were employees of the Vertical Club, then the most high-end health club in the United States. Many young Latino men held jobs as housekeeping and porter staff there. Mickey Z. worked at Vertical for several years, rising up to the position of gym floor manager.

"Over time, the housekeeping staff evolved into something of a family affair. One porter—I'll call him Neil—got hired first. He was part of a large Honduran community in the Bronx. Little by little, as job slots opened, Neil would suggest family members (or friends) from his neighborhood. This resulted in a tight-knit group that took their work seriously and looked out for each other... one night I got a call at home from a co-worker named Rafael... Rafael was Latino and from the Bronx so he also became tight with the porters and often helped me with translating... Anyway, when I picked up the phone on the evening of March 27, 1990, I heard Rafael's somber voice: 'Mick, I think we've got a big problem.'"

Four of the 87 victims were porters on the Vertical Club housekeeping staff, all young men, one still in high school. And they weren't coming back to work, that day or ever. And for Bronx residents contemplating the meaning of this tragedy, there was rich and bitter irony inherent in the fact that so many of those who had died had held low-wage jobs serving the New York elite, those same rich white folks who were displaying a measure of satisfied indifference in their handling of the tragedy.

The disaster left in its wake a chain of devastated relatives all the way from the streets of East Tremont to the towns and villages of Honduras. And once the identification of the dead was complete, the official mourning would begin, a process stretching over several days.

It began at the school, where the state Crime Victims Compensation Board were arranging payments to families for funeral arrangements and for the return of the bodies of several victims to Honduras. In another room at the school, officials were returning the belongings of victims retrieved from the scene to their relatives.

Concepcion Matos, 34 years old, opened up a manila envelope containing what her brother had been carrying when he died: his wallet, a key, $6, a once-soggy napkin and a letter with a Honduran postmark.

"There is a wave of realization of death again after a period of calm," said Ken Curtin, director of the Red Cross disaster relief team. "When people see property that belonged to their loved ones, they sometimes realize the finality of the entire disaster. It's very tough stuff."

From there the mourners dispersed to several local funeral homes, including the LaPaz, at 285 East 149th Street, the Rafael Ortiz funeral home several blocks away, and Rivera's at Bathgate. The enormity of the tragedy had overtaxed the resources of many of these providers, who had to hire additional space to accommodate such an unanticipated glut of coffins and mourners. Rivera's made use of a spare room in the neighboring community building for seven coffins that would not fit in the main home.

On March 28, the grieving queued in long lines behind police barricades as they waited to enter one or other of several chapels in the Bronx that had been booked for memorial services. The commemorations continued past sundown. The largest began at Rivera's, where a procession carried seventeen coffins across the street to a service held in St. Joseph's Roman Catholic Church. Reverend Henry Mills gave a tear-filled sermon as mothers and fathers collapsed in the pews. "We pray this evening that the Lord may strengthen our understanding. We hope the Lord eternal will lead them to his home!" he said.

Afterwards, many friends and relatives of the dead remained standing in the street outside, singing hymns and whispering prayers as the coffins were returned to Rivera's. A truck with rotating spotlights was hired to cast light beams into the night sky, so the remembrances could go on through the evening.

The coffin of Elias Colon was held for viewing at the Rafael Ortiz funeral home. Despite the fact that it was now widely believed that it was his negligence and complacency that had contributed to the severity of the fire, scores of mourners visited to pay tribute to the proprietor of Happy Land. Mr. Colon's widow, Elena, one of the few who had survived, sat in an antechamber and tearfully accepted the condolences of friends, loved ones and well-wishers.

Around the neighborhoods of the west Bronx, photographs of the victims appeared everywhere, on doors, shop windows, and taped to mailboxes. And in front of Happy Land itself, where shrouded bodies had once lined the pavement, a collection of flowers and mementos of the dead steadily gathered in an attempt by the aggrieved to bring back something of meaning and beauty from a tragedy that was, for them, unmatched in its senseless cruelty.

The rituals by which western peoples commemorate death—funerals, masses, wakes and the like—are often somber, quiet and stately affairs. But the mourning process after Happy Land was nothing like that. These folks grieved like Central Americans, not white Americans. There was no self-consciousness, no attempt to be dignified in grief. Instead, everywhere on the streets, there was an almost palpable sense of rage and heartbreak. The people literally lay down on the steps before St. Thomas Aquinas Church, weeping. As the processions traveled down the streets of west Bronx, convulsive wails of agony could be heard, breaking out from the crowd.

The grief of this community was visceral and confronting. Beamed into the lounge rooms of Americans everywhere, it was a spectacle that inspired feelings not only of sympathy for a community that had until that time remained largely hidden—but unease, maybe even shame.

To gain a full appreciation of why this event was so shocking to so many people, one must remember that amongst the sheathed bodies that were laid out on the sidewalk outside the club that morning of March 25 were visibly small ones—the bodies of youngsters barely into their teens. These horrific images appeared in newspapers and TV news reports, along with the grimmest details and speculations about the brutal manner in which they had died. Even the most hard-nosed and unsympathetic observers—those that might otherwise have held the view that immigrants, some of whom were without residential rights, attending an unsafe illegal nightclub were deserving of whatever fate came their way—had trouble accepting that innocent kids "had it coming". In this way, amongst others, the Happy Land tragedy would cast a new, stark light on the hidden complexities of immigration and multiculturalism in New York.

How was it that these overlooked, vulnerable people had been compelled to exist in such desperate, sub-standard conditions that they came to die in that way? And who was really to blame?

"The fire stunned the city and the nation for its circumstances and the sheer number of victims," wrote Robert E. Tomasson for the *New York Times*. In the aftermath of the disaster, a sense of public outrage built day after day, with each new revelation.

Because the fact that this was the worst mass murder in U.S. history had brought a great measure of notoriety to this incident, for the first time, Central American immigrant communities in New York had the attention of mainstream white America. And donations and financial assistance began pouring in. Social agencies organized payment for funerals and counseling for the relatives of victims.

But the real compensation, many felt—the kind that would enable the survival of families who had lost sole breadwinners, for example—had to come from the wealthy, negligent landlords—and that such would come to pass was still far from certain.

* * *

Lydia Feliciano returned to the gymnasium at Public School 57 on Monday, March 27, this time to enquire about financial aid for friends who had lost relatives in the fire.

It had been an awful couple of days for Feliciano. Since the fire, she had spent as much time as possible at home, hiding herself away. Not only had she lost her niece and many friends and colleagues from the club, but she had become the target of wrath and condemnation from her own community after the press revealed that it was her former partner, Julio Gonzalez, who had started the fire—and that she had survived.

Dressed conservatively in a calf-length dress, low-rise black heels and a black overcoat with a leopard print collar, she took a deep breath as she entered the grounds, steeling herself for what was likely to come.

Several of the mourners spun around, pointing, yanking the shirtsleeves of their companions.

"Look! It's her!" they said, casting wide-eyed, outraged glances at each other.

Edgardo Rodriguez, 22 years old, had come to the school that day to seek financial assistance from the Red Cross for the return of the bodies of four of his relatives to their native Honduras.

"I can't believe she is here!" he cried. "How can she show her face?"

Soon a small mob was gathering around Feliciano, backing her up against a brick wall, blocking her access to the Red Cross table. They fired a series of questions and recriminations at her.

Toli Gutierez, 33, got in Feliciano's face, raising her finger.

"May I ask you something? What are you doing here?"

Feliciano tried to defend herself. "I lost people too!" she cried in outrage. But the angry rabble, which had now swelled to around 20 people, weren't having any of it.

A recurring question revolved around the service entryway, which had apparently become blocked at some stage after the fire started. Some believed that Feliciano had left the gate down after she escaped, but this is unlikely, as Phillip Figueroa had also escaped through that door.

Gutierez persisted:

"How did you get out, no one else got out? Who closed the gate?"

Feliciano said she jumped through the flame in the doorway just as it was spreading. She and Argueta had struggled with the gate; they barely got through. She was in such a hurry to get away, she sure as hell never pulled down the gate. She didn't know how the service entryway came to be blocked.

"How could you leave? How could you do that? How can you even show your face here?" demanded Rodriguez.

The crowd's rancor was now drawing the attention of police ranged around the exits. They broke up the melee and escorted Feliciano away.

Human nature is nothing if not perverse. Surely Feliciano should have been deserving of some sympathy—after all, her former partner had tried to kill her, and as a result of his actions, she had lost her niece, her friends and her job and had only narrowly escaped death herself. And yet, as prosecutor Eric Warner later said, "People treated Lydia like she was the cause; she wasn't."

Why did they blame her? There were many reasons, some at least minimally rational, others not so much. After the disaster, the people were drowning in a tidal wave of anguish and anger; an excess of tormenting emotion that they became eager to displace on any handy target. What better target than the one who had survived, when their loved ones were lost? Her continuing existence inspired resentment.

So few had lived; the fact that she had drew suspicion, in much the same way as the detectives had initially been suspicious of Phillip Figueroa.

There were the claims that she did not do enough to alert others of the danger when the fire started, instead choosing to save herself—and to hell with the rest. The fact that she had disappeared into the night without telling anyone. The possibility that she might have been afraid of her would-be killer did not really register or garner much compassion.

Maybe the biggest reason of all was rooted in good old-fashioned sexism. There were those who said the whole thing could have been avoided if she had just gone back with Gonzalez, or never left him in the first place. The social milieu of the time and place was not particularly hospitable to the notion of female self-determination, and certainly not to the idea that a woman might exchange her partner for "other men."

Instead of placing the blame squarely on Gonzalez for acting on his murderous impulses, they blamed Feliciano for provoking him. Nowhere in this narrative was there any sense that a woman had a right to leave a man or break things off if she was unhappy. Instead, these critics bought into Gonzalez's own justification for his behavior: he owned her; "she was his woman."

Following the disaster, columnist Jimmy Breslin spoke with an associate of Gonzalez and Feliciano, a guy named Jesus. Jesus said Feliciano was a troublemaker: "She never should have told him to go away when he came to the club." Feliciano was so clearly in the wrong, he said, that "people in the Bronx" wondered why Gonzalez "didn't just borrow a gun and shoot her," instead of burning the club down.

Feliciano's victimization in the wake of the tragedy did not end there. She was immediately enrolled in witness protection, which was not necessary so much to protect her from Gonzalez's associates as from the surviving friends and relatives of those who had perished in the fire—many of them neighbors, former friends and acquaintances.

At the trial, she was always escorted to and from the court under heavy guard. At the behest of the judge, surviving loved ones gathered in the gallery mostly kept their composure, but her appearances were always met with angry, disapproving stares.

Not long after, she moved away from West Farms altogether—the blame and condemnation from neighbors was too much to bear; she needed a fresh start amongst people who would not judge her about things of which they clearly had no understanding.

Chapter 10

During a preliminary hearing held on November 15 before Justice Burton B. Roberts in Bronx Supreme Court, there was less than welcome news for the relatives of the unfortunate souls who had died in the Happy Land fire.

Richard W. Berne, appointed defense lawyer for Julio Gonzalez, confirmed that he would be pursuing an insanity defense on behalf of his client.

Gonzalez had indeed confessed to the crime and at no time did he renounce responsibility for the act of setting the fire, but it was the conviction of both himself and his lawyer that he was not morally responsible for the 87 deaths due to his state of mind at the time of the crime. The defense was one of "temporary insanity," which held that Gonzalez "was not criminally responsible because of mental defect," as Berne stated. Berne had, during the prior month, filed motions indicating he would use the results of psychiatric examinations on his client.

There was not too much to be surprised about here. Temporary insanity is a well-worn defense in cases of crimes of passion and murders resulting from domestic violence situations. It holds that the defendant was insane during the commission of a crime, but somehow regained their sanity after the criminal act was carried out. "Something bad got into me, the devil got into me!" as Gonzalez had said, distancing himself from personal responsibility for his crime.

The defendant's choice to pursue an insanity defense, and the possibility that he might consequently escape fair and due punishment, deeply angered the loved ones of the victims. They loudly vented their fury against Gonzalez and swore that even if he were found criminally culpable, no punishment or term of sentence would ever be sufficient.

"The justice he's going to get is not what he deserves," said Tracey Stovall, whose friend, Denny Alvarez, was among the victims. "A thousand years, two thousand years—nothing is enough!"

The offense was aggravated by the fact that even if Gonzalez was convicted for the worst mass murder in American history, he would only serve 25 to life because the sentences under New York law would be concurrent.

While a pall of uncertainty hung over Gonzalez's punishment, it also became clear during the hearing that the victims' families might also be unable to seek justice in the form of penalties against the building's owners of leaseholders or financial recompense from those parties.

Bronx District Attorney Robert T. Johnson said that the building's owner, Alex DiLorenzo, and Jay Weiss and Morris Jaffe, who were the leaseholders and managing agents, bore no criminal liability for the deaths or for the safety violations at the club. Mr. Elias Colon, who died in the fire, "was involved in the construction and operation of the club in violation of building codes and other safety considerations, and... his obligations made him directly responsible for the condition of the premises." On the other hand, there was no evidence that Mr. DiLorenzo "ever visited the club or had any personal knowledge of its physical plant." Notices of minor violations, like the lack of an assembly permit, were sent to the companies of all three, and Mr. Weiss and Mr. Jaffe began an eviction proceeding against Mr. Colon. Mr. Johnson said, however, that there was no evidence that the three knew about more serious safety violations.

For many onlookers, the fact that the owners and leaseholders simply "didn't know" about the problems at Happy Land should not have exempted them from responsibility. Prosecutor Johnson did in fact take time out of his statement to issue a worthy-sounding critique of the phenomenon of "absentee landlords" who raked in cash from their stake in city buildings while taking no interest in their safety, fitness for purpose or day-to-day operation.

"It is painfully obvious that the operation of this social club under the attendant conditions was, in a very real sense, a disaster waiting to happen. It is equally obvious that the safety violations in the club were by no means a secret and that the private parties and city officials could have been more diligent in their response."

It was a common problem in New York. Wealthy, out-of-touch property moguls such as DiLorenzo bought up blocks and blocks of buildings in parts of New York they personally wouldn't deign to set foot in, such as East Tremont.

The owners happily enjoyed their profits but barely stayed in touch with the leaseholders and were more concerned about decreasing liability than the safety of occupants.

In a moral sense, Johnson clearly regarded the situation as unfortunate, but the fact remained, there was simply no mechanism under the law by which they could be held accountable.

So if there was to be no restitution from criminal prosecution of the defendant, nor the owners, then from where?

Eighty-seven dead. It seemed unfathomable that nobody would be held responsible, but the possibility loomed and weighed heavily on the minds and hearts of those left behind.

* * *

Jury selection continued through the months of April and June, and the case finally came to trial in July 1991. The courtroom was densely packed with the friends and relatives of the victims, who alternately wept and stared with expressions of white-eyed anger during parts of the proceedings that were less than respectful to their grief.

As predicted, defense counsel entirely left alone the issue of who started the fire. Between the discovery of the gasoline container at the scene, Gonzalez's gasoline-soaked shoes and clothing, and the testimony of Lydia Feliciano, gas station attendant Edward Porros, and others at the club who had witnessed arguments between Feliciano and Gonzalez and Gonzalez and the bouncer, Gonzalez's culpability as the instigator of the attack was beyond question, and it was simply not open to find him innocent on any evidential or circumstantial grounds. And then, of course, there was the most damning evidence of all, Gonzalez's own unambiguous confession.

The defense of last resort therefore had to be one referring to state of mind. Such was made clear by defense attorney Richard Berne's opening statement:

"Ladies and gentlemen, on March 25, 1990, Julio Gonzalez started the fire in the Happyland [sic] Social Club. You've all heard me concede that repeatedly. I'm conceding that he started the fire, I'm conceding that 87 people died as a result of that fire, no question as to who they were, no question as to how they died, no question that it was a horrible tragedy, almost beyond human imagination... but ladies and gentlemen, when Julio Gonzalez started that fire, he was legally insane. I'm using the term insane, you know the legal expression.

That is the only issue I have addressed so far during *voir dire*, it's the only issue I'm addressing now, it's the only issue I will address with evidence during the trial, the only issue you will hear me refer to in my summation, it is the only issue I think you need seriously consider when you retire to deliberate."

Over the course of the proceeding, Berne rounded out his argument, such as it was. He pointed to the fact that Gonzalez had shown remorse for his actions; he had cried on the bus home, at Carmen Melendez's apartment, and during his confession. Given his remorse, it made sense that he was a "normal" or near-normal individual, capable of empathy, who had surely not been in his right mind at the time of the crime. Gonzalez, he charged, had suffered a "psychotic break" during which he carried out the attack against the club. The theory that the defendant had lost contact with reality was, according to counsel, supported by a history of mental illness.

"Don't judge Julio Gonzalez by the standards of your own mind," he stated. "He doesn't have your mind."

Temporary insanity defenses have often been successful historically in similar cases because people are reluctant to accept that individuals intentionally hurt or kill their intimates, especially when such individuals appear to be otherwise peaceful and law-abiding individuals.

If the person seems capable of remorse and empathy, or is a respectable member of the community, the theory goes that something must have gone wrong with their mind for a brief time, that accounts for their actions. In recent years a body of research has grown showing that mental illness defenses in cases of domestic violence are, more often than not, spurious. The researchers note that men who batter women are usually quite capable of handling themselves and being non-violent when interacting with authorities; the violent behavior is reserved for their intimates and almost always occurs behind closed doors. The explanation is not that they "lose their minds" or lose their cool; it is because the violence is intentional and part of a control structure they implement over their partner and the relationship.

But Gonzalez, Berne said, had undergone extensive evaluation whilst sequestered in Bellevue Hospital in the period leading up to trial, and those assessments showed that even if he had started the fire, he was innocent in the moral and legal sense. The attorney brought in two forensic psychologists detailing the findings of the assessments, Gonzalez's alleged history of mental illness, and how and why it led to Gonzalez setting fire to Happy Land.

The substance of the expert testimony of the two psychologists was that Gonzalez suffered a mental defect in the psychotic or schizophrenic class, and that while he had periods of normal cognitive functioning, he tended to experience relapses of his condition during periods of acute emotional stress. The experts stated that Gonzalez had "heard voices" commanding him to set the fire and that he felt a "force" compelling him to commit the crime. Both had noted Gonzalez's habit of talking to himself regularly—a habit, they said, that derived from his propensity to hear voices. They proposed that an imaginary persecutor or "guardian angel" had ordered him to set fire to the club. They also pointed to the possibility that Gonzalez had suffered a brain injury from a fall he experienced as a child, which had affected his mental state intermittently throughout his life. Irrespective of any injury, the defendant was "intellectually limited" and had an IQ of only 79.

It was even possible that the "force" directing him to commit the crime had been the phantom of Gonzalez's deceased grandmother. Clinical psychologist Roy Aranda, the first witness called by the defense, said Gonzalez told him he had seen a vision of his dead grandmother while awaiting trial in prison and that she "told him all is forgiven and not to worry." That the defendant saw "visions" was held up as further evidence that he was afflicted by some form of psychotic illness, the characteristic symptoms of which are visual and auditory hallucinations.

Prosecutor Eric Warner was harshly dismissive of the claims.

"Voices? That sounds pretty darn phony. Forces? It sounds like Star Wars," he said.

The prosecution team brought in their own forensic psychiatrist on August 13 to rebut the expert testimony of the defense. Robert Berger, an associate professor of psychiatry at New York University and deputy director of the forensic psychiatry unit at Bellevue Hospital Center, stated that Gonzalez exhibited certain psychopathologies, but these were not of the psychotic type and did not impinge on his cognition or reasoning.

The defendant, he conceded, had "experienced periods of alcohol abuse [and had] borderline antisocial personality features... and borderline mental function." These, however, were not mental disorders in the sense that the defense was presenting it. They did not impact the defendant's ability to judge right from wrong, nor did they "compel" him to do anything; the attack was rationally orchestrated and implemented by Gonzalez himself.

Further, Berger contended, individuals suffering from psychotic illnesses usually require hospitalization for periods, and there was no record of Gonzalez spending time in a mental institution before he had committed the crime and threatened to commit suicide. The "history" of mental illness was fictitious.

Even if, for argument's sake, Gonzalez had experienced a psychotic break, it was highly unlikely that he would have had the executive planning ability in that state to carry out the very specific steps that led him to dump the gasoline in the inner door of Happy Land.

People who hear voices, Berger stated, do not generally receive detailed instructions on how to act. In this instance, the defendant had acted in a way consistent with criminal premeditation, not an irrational or impulsive state of mind. Such was shown by the fact that Gonzalez:

- had asked the gas station attendant for $1 worth of gasoline because he only had a dollar to spend

- had lied to the attendant about having a car breakdown when initially refused the purchase, and

- Had waited for patrons outside the club to disperse before he went in and doused the entrance area with gasoline.

Berger contextualized Gonzalez's actions within a framework of character rather than mental defect. Gonzalez was "an individual who has a tendency to be more concerned with his own needs and desires than those of other people." He had a history of making "spur-of-the-moment decisions," such as eloping with a woman in Cuba just because he was late bringing her home from a party. But he "doesn't have an impairment in his sense of reality, in his relationship with reality and his ability to test that reality." Further, "ignoring consequences is not equal to not appreciating the consequences," Berger said.

Lydia Feliciano's testimony also cast doubt on the defense's key argument. She told the court that Gonzalez "tended to be a jealous individual, [and] when he got jealous, he got angry." She described her altercation with Gonzalez at the club less than an hour before the attack took place and testified that he had issued specific threats, saying "You're not going to work here anymore. I told you and I swear it."

Phillip Figueroa also reported back to the court the fact that he had heard arguing between Feliciano and Gonzalez at around 2 a.m. when he entered the club and that he had heard Gonzalez threatening the bouncer shortly before the attack: "You will pay for it!"

Taking up this thread of argument, Eric Warner told the jury it was clear that there was a specific motive for the arson that made a mockery of the concept of an irrational outburst or a "psychotic break." It was not mental illness that prompted Gonzalez but jealousy and humiliation over being jilted by a former girlfriend.

"This defendant didn't lose his sanity, he lost his temper ... He had enough intellectual capacity to know what he was doing. He was making very specific and clear threats."

The jury were also given the opportunity to view the videotape containing Gonzalez's confession to police made on the day of his arrest. Certainly that confession was unequivocal and left no doubt that Gonzalez was taking responsibility for the arson attack; but elements of it also made doubtful the proposition that the confessor was in an impaired state of mind either at the time or during the crime. While Gonzalez had sobbed intermittently throughout, he was demonstrably lucid and constructed a thorough accounting of his movements on the night. He clearly described the motive as jealousy, mentioning that he recalled asking Feliciano if she had a lot of suitors. "Then she told me, yes, that she had a lot," he said. "That was when I got angry."

He recounted how he was kicked out of the club and how he had conceived of the plan to set fire to the club. Mr. Gonzalez's first impulse upon being kicked out of Happy Land was "to close the club" by "calling the police" because he thought it was an illegal establishment, he said. Instead, he decided to burn it. "There I lost my mind," he said. He described walking to the gas station, talking the attendant into selling him gasoline, and dropping the matches only after patrons milling outside the club had left.

The videotape contained certain statements that were meant to lend credence to the idea that Gonzalez had "gone mad." He said he had lost his mind, did not know what he was doing, repeatedly cried and was told by others (his friend Arturo Martinez and neighbor Yvonne Torres) that he was crazy for doing what he did. But the overriding impression yielded by the tape was of Gonzalez's vindictiveness and the deliberate nature of his actions. There was also this statement, which was utterly suggestive of a calculated and planning mindset on the part of the defendant: "I knew that I was going to do damage but not of that intensity."

As at his arraignment and in previous hearings, Gonzalez showed little emotion during the trial. He sat slumped in his chair, his head barely visible above the defense table, occasionally glancing up at the judge and his interpreter. From time to time he leaned his forehead into his hands and jiggled one foot under the table. During the showing of his videotaped confession, however, several of those present noticed his eyes blinking rapidly.

In the time from the fire up until trial, commentators had differed sharply about whether Gonzalez was truly sorry for his crime or even appreciated the magnitude of what he had done. Berne had, as we have seen, made much of the significance of his repeated episodes of crying. Police Lieutenant Raymond O'Donnell told the press without a shred of hesitation, "He is remorseful. He has been crying." Carmen Melendez told the court how he had sat at the foot of her bed, screaming and crying, when he arrived at her apartment in the early hours of the morning and confessed to starting the fire. Warner, on the other hand, later said that he "was looking at a person who did not display any emotion for killing anyone, much less that many people."

There was the fact that Gonzalez had at one time evidently considered not surrendering and running away; this was shown by the fact that during his initial conversation with Arturo Martinez, he hadn't admitted to setting the fire and only did so when told by his friend that there was no chance he was going to get away with it. Most damning of all, many said, was the fact that he was sleeping when police went to apprehend him.

The man at the center of the story was surely an enigma. For the friends and relatives of the victims who had traveled from as far as Honduras and Puerto Rico to see justice done, he was to be spared no compassion: he was "the monster."

For others, including Berne and some detectives who had worked the case, Gonzalez aroused more ambivalent feelings. To them, the man responsible for 87 brutal killings seemed so very broken and pathetic they had a hard time hating him for what he had done. No matter the gravity of his crime, his personal history, his plight and the desperation of his circumstances in the lead up to the fire inspired—of all emotions—sadness, maybe even compassion.

Psychologists and social theorists increasingly make the observation that male violence against women is often specifically rooted in the experience of shame and humiliation. When a man feels most powerless is when he strikes hardest. Although his crime was atrocious, Gonzalez's story contained so many relatable elements that over time, have become part of the media narrative of the victimized male: job loss, loss of status as a provider, loss of children, rejection by a woman. In our culture and society, the narrative is put forward to explain how ordinary men come to do very bad things.

His defense lawyer, Richard Berne, seemed to feel that Gonzalez was fundamentally a good and ordinary man. And this was why, as in so many similar cases before and more to come after, the defense had resorted to the argument that he "must have gone crazy."

Look, Berne pleaded to the jury in his closing argument, this is a good, normal man. His actions must have been an aberration, the result of a brief sojourn into madness:

"When you first heard about this case, that as a result of an argument with a girlfriend or a bouncer, that a man would go and buy a dollar's worth of gas and burn down a club and kill 87 people, I bet you said, 'This man must be crazy'. You have a man with a serious underlying mental defect. It's a lifelong problem... It is so easy to make fun of it. How can it be: He was a psychotic that night, he wasn't a psychotic the next day? But those kind of psychotic breaks are brief."

In truth, the morality of ordinary men is ambiguous and inconsistent. Ordinary men are capable of violence as well as remorse. They are capable of crying for their sins, and then denying committing them. The crime that Gonzalez committed, when viewed alongside his tears and his history as a timid, kind man who helped his neighbors, did not need to be explained with reference to madness.

Berne's closing remarks showed just how weak the defense's position really was. For the explanation for violence committed by "ordinary men," which posits that such violence must be an act of "temporary madness" when the man who committed it is *so clearly* a good and ordinary person, always has been and always will be a circular argument: an argument which commits the logical fallacy of assuming what it is attempting to prove. Just because Gonzalez was an ordinary man, it did not mean he was innocent.

The jury, on this occasion, didn't buy it. While the trial had dragged on for four long, emotional weeks—weeks during which Justice Burton Roberts had repeatedly had to ask friends and relatives of the victims to leave the courtroom when they burst into tears—the jury returned its verdict after just three days of deliberations.

On August 19, 1991, Julio Gonzalez was found guilty of 174 counts of murder, two for each victim, and one count each of first-degree arson and first-degree assault.

Relatives of the victims smiled and wept when they heard jury foreman Luis Rodriguez pronounce the word "guilty" 176 times, but they remained quiet, as ordered by Roberts.

"God is great. He was guilty—we knew he was guilty," said a woman spectator.

While the verdict itself was mostly seen by those left behind as extremely fair and just, sentencing was always going to be a sore point.

Sentencing was scheduled for September 19. On the day, Gonzalez was once again stony and silent as Judge Roberts gave him the stiffest punishment allowable under the law: 25 years to life for each victim. The harshness of the sentence was unparalleled in New York history, but in practice, there was always the chance that Gonzalez would go free after 25 years, since in that state any sentence for an act committed during a single offense had to be served concurrently, not consecutively.

Bronx District Attorney Robert Johnson said 25 years to life was "inadequate and unjust given the magnitude of this crime."

Johnson also remarked that he supported legislation that would allow consecutive sentences for each death in cases where a single criminal act claims the life of more than one victim, but that without such a law, 25 years to life in prison was the most that could be imposed on Gonzalez.

The survivors and relatives did not care to understand the intricacies of the law. Whatever the statutes said, on the face of it, 25 years was an absurdly light penalty for a crime of this magnitude—the worst mass murder in American history. Most said that ideally Gonzalez would have received the death penalty, and failing that, life behind bars might be barely adequate.

Karen Gamoneda, who lost her two brothers-in-law, expressed the views of many:

"It should be more than that. He took 87 lives. He should pay with his."

Postscript

Julio Gonzalez lived out his remaining days at the Clinton Correctional Facility in Dannemora, New York.

However remorseful he might have appeared the day after the crime, his later actions showed him to be unwilling to accept punishment. In August 1991, he unsuccessfully tried to appeal his conviction on the grounds that detectives had been heavy-handed during his arrest and had intimidated him into confessing, accusations which, as we have seen, were patently untrue.

In December of 1993, he again filed a motion to vacate his convictions on the basis that the People did not supply the audiotapes made by the medical examiners who performed the 87 autopsies conducted as a result of the fire. While, given his confession, those tapes might be considered irrelevant to the judicial determination, the defendant contended that the tapes were Rosario material and the People were required to obtain the audiotapes from the Office of the Chief Medical Examiner (OCME) and to provide them to the defense. He was thus suggesting that procedural irregularities had occurred which indicated "bad faith" and invalidated the court's ultimate findings. The motion was denied.

Gonzalez received disciplinary actions for possession of drugs and weapons during the first decade of his imprisonment, but after 2000, there was no disciplinary action taken against him, and he was hopeful for parole.

In 2015 he was eligible for his first hearing. Again, Gonzalez minimized his moral culpability in the disaster, this time claiming that "the anger was towards the man who had me leave," not Lydia Feliciano or those inside the club. He said that the bouncer had threatened to hit him, "and I told him I was going to leave, but I was coming back." When he set the fire, he said, "at that moment I wasn't thinking about what I was doing." And regarding the club, he "didn't realize how many people were inside. When I got there, there were some people there, but, you know, there were two floors there. I didn't know that there were two floors in that place."

That latter statement, at a minimum, was demonstrably untrue, as Gonzalez had been seen upstairs on the night of the fire.

Parole was denied, with the board finding that Gonzalez was likely to re-offend given his lack of remorse. He "would not live at liberty without again violating the law," and his release would be "incompatible with the welfare of society."

A factor contributing to the decision, though on a lower level of importance, was that Gonzalez had done nothing to prepare himself for life outside. The prison's programs offered him the possibility to learn English and to gain his GED, but he had taken up neither opportunity. He had not reached out to any community organizations to help him find work once he was released and had very poor prospects of finding employment. When asked how he would support himself, Gonzalez mentioned "a woman he had met on the internet" would be willing to take him in.

In all, it appeared that if released, Gonzalez planned to live much in the way he had before he set fire to the club—as a rootless parasite dependent on the graces of a woman. Since it was his desperate condition after losing his only means of survival in the form of Lydia Feliciano that had led up to the tragedy and had in part motivated the crime, the board deemed that a risk in itself.

Gonzalez was eligible for parole again in 2016, but he didn't survive to make the hearing. On September 13, 2016, he suffered a heart attack in his cell. He was removed to nearby Champlain Valley Physicians Hospital in Plattsburg, New York, but died a short time later.

"He did not die of regret," remarked a reporter for the *New York Daily News*.

* * *

Although the Bronx Supreme Court ruled that the owner and landlord of the building that housed Happy Land were in no way criminally responsible for the deaths that resulted from the fire, those parties ultimately accrued a fairly harsh financial penalty for the attitude of benign negligence that had meant the fire was much more deadly than it might otherwise have been.

There is no way of knowing how many lives might have been spared had these men taken a more active interest in the amenity and safety of the building.

The New York City Corporation Counsel finally filed misdemeanor charges against DiLorenzo and Weiss. The charges were filed on the basis that they were partially responsible for building code violations caused by their tenant. DiLorenzo and Weiss pleaded guilty in May 1992. The terms of the penalty agreement included community service and a fine of $150,000. The proceeds of the fine were supposedly earmarked for the development of a Bronx community center for Hondurans; however, as you will learn below, that center was never ultimately built.

There was also a lawsuit filed by the relatives of victims against DiLorenzo, Weiss, the City, and certain manufacturers of unsafe building materials that had been used in the construction of the club. That suit was filed at the outset for the staggering sum of $5 billion but was ultimately settled in July 1995 for $15.8 million or $163,000 per victim. The reduced sum was agreed in recognition of financial "difficulties" into which Weiss had fallen by the middle of the decade.

* * *

Funds from the compensation pool were earmarked for the creation of the Memorial to the Eighty-Seven. In a small park across the street from 1959 Southern Boulevard, the site of the now vanished Happy Land club, stands a rose granite obelisk designed by architects Steve de Noyer, Claire Dudley and José Antonio Velásquez, and inscribed with the names of each of the victims of that deadly fire of March 25, 1990.

The dedication reads: "In memory of the 87 men and women who lost their lives in the Happy Land Social Club fire at 1959 Southern Blvd. West of this site on March 25, 1990. Dedicated 1995. May they all be happy in eternity. Although we cannot see them, forever they will be a beautiful part of our hearts' memory."

Here, family members and friends of the victims visit and place flowers on special occasions such as birthdays, holidays and anniversaries. There are also annual commemoration services held at the site, with masses conducted in one or other of the local Catholic churches.

Although we are now thirty years away from the disaster, the annual commemorations continue to draw large and enthusiastic crowds. In 2018, hundreds of Bronx residents turned out for a mass at Saint Thomas Aquinas Church located at 1900 Crotona Parkway at 1 p.m., followed by a procession from Saint

Thomas Aquinas Church towards the monument at East Tremont Avenue, between Southern Boulevard and Crotona Parkway, for a rosary and candlelight vigil.

Lydia Feliciano, who moved to the other side of the Bronx after the disaster to get away from blame, did her grieving in private. She has never participated in any of the public memorial gatherings, since she feared that showing her face would provoke the same aggression and outrage from other mourners she experienced all those years ago at Public School 57.

Two decades later, Feliciano was in a nursing home, on dialysis, and recovering from open heart surgery. She said that it was sad that she could not join the community in their mourning, nor share her grief with them. But the fact that she had been blamed for the fire, when she was only trying to survive the actions of the man who was truly responsible, made her feel less kindly towards many former friends and associates—so, ultimately, she wasn't missing much, as they were simply not the people she thought they were. She did not wish to encounter them again at all. Due to her isolation from her community, she has largely had to endure her suffering, and recover from the tragedy, alone and without social support.

Phillip Figueroa experienced his own struggles after the fire and eventually returned to his hometown of Trujillo in Honduras to forget the sounds of screaming and the blaring sirens of the Bronx which were forever a reminder of that dark night. As a key witness, and initially a suspect, he was monitored by detectives for months afterwards. He suffered from post-traumatic stress and severe insomnia and restlessness, both as a result of his involvement in the investigation and trial and the aftereffects of the night itself. Amongst the cadavers lined up on the pavement that morning, he had recognized six friends from Trujillo and eleven acquaintances from the nearby Garifuna community Limón.

Phillip's remarkable story of survival was featured in the New York papers, and as a result, he attained a sudden and unexpected measure of celebrity. He later recalled strangers approaching him on the street asking him for his autograph. He actually didn't enjoy all this newfound attention. Always a humble man who had largely kept to himself, he was completely unused to it; moreover, the fire had been a dreadful and harrowing experience for him, not a source of excitement or morbid curiosity, as it seemed to be for those who approached him on the street.

After returning to Trujillo, Phillip eked out a barebones existence by selling home-made maracas and knock-off wallets on the streets. Eventually, he received word that he would get $9,000 in compensation from the funds seized from the building owners for survivors and relatives. The catch was that he had to return to the United States to claim the payment.

He set out on a ten-hour bus trip to the Honduran capital Tegucigalpa to apply for a visa at the US Embassy so he could collect his money in New York. He explained his situation to the embassy officers and told them his intentions of immediately returning to Trujillo after collecting the money. The US embassy refused his visa application. They also turned him down on two subsequent applications.

Phillip then decided to make the risky move of entering the US illegally, travelling with a friend's visa and passport. He didn't want to do it, but he was desperate for the money and felt he deserved it for all the misfortune and trauma he had suffered. He arrived in Louisiana by plane and was immediately detained and imprisoned for six months.

"I nearly died in prison," he later said. He still suffered claustrophobia and shell-shock after the fire, and he was kept in a confined cell.

Eventually, while in jail, he finally received some of the compensation he was promised. Law firm Smith and Smith of New York sent him a check for $6,000, keeping $3,000 for themselves as a service fee. Phillip was deported back to Honduras as just another unwanted illegal immigrant. His story, then, presented a number of ironies. As an online interview with Figueroa noted, "Phillip went from being a national hero on the cover of the New York Times to being another deported Honduran resigned to hustling on the sidewalk of his hometown".

In 1998, large parts of Honduras, including Trujillo and the capital Tegucigalpa, were devastated by Hurricane Mitch, which caused the worst flooding to strike the nation in the twentieth century. The president of Honduras stated that the storm had set the country back fifty years in terms of economic development. The storm wrecked about 35,000 houses and damaged another 50,000, leaving up to 1.5 million people homeless, or about 20 percent of the country's population. Honduras is still recovering and dreading the possible or maybe inevitable arrival of another hurricane of similar strength. Meanwhile, more and more immigrants from Honduras are arriving in the United States: their crops are failing due to increasing temperatures and drought, and they are running out of food and livelihood. As of 2019, Honduras joins other nations including Nicaragua, Iraq, Yemen, Venezuela, Sudan and Libya on the world list of failed states. Many of its remaining inhabitants intend to leave or are in the process of leaving.

Ruben Valladares endured a long and painful recovery after the fire, both physically and emotionally. He underwent a series of skin graft surgeries, which were difficult but ultimately very successful; today, as his friend Phillip Figueroa remarked, he "looks really terrific."

Unlike Figueroa, Valladares remained in the United States, although he travels to Honduras frequently. Every year he takes part in the commemoration services.

Describing his life and his journey since the night of the fire, he told a Honduran news service, "For me it is still as if it happened today. I feel like it's the first day: it's something I have not been able to assimilate yet. I have too many memories of that night. It's something terrible I have to live with and it's worse when I remember my friends who were talking to me and could not leave. Many of the employees [of Happy Land] became family and I could tell you that of the 87 people that died, 15 were very close to me."

Ruben Valladares works in the boating industry, selling products to other boats in nearby waters. He says that despite everything, he tries, and mostly succeeds, at living a normal life. "I managed to make myself a home, and I have four children, and a beautiful family."

When Valladares was interviewed in 2015, the subject of Gonzalez's imminent parole hearing came up. Valladares did not believe he was remorseful no matter how many tears the man had shed and was adamant that he should never be released.

"For me, that man must remain in prison for the rest of his life. He does not deserve to leave. I ask the authorities to deny him probation. That person is not good for society, is a harmful individual that can represent a danger to the community." Fortunately for Valladares, Gonzalez died just one year after this interview.

Despite the fact that compensation for relatives was ultimately secured by legally enforced financial sanctions against the building's owners, those left behind faced an uncertain future in the interim and oftentimes much further into the future. The Happy Land disaster made widows of nearly two dozen women. The vast majority of the victims had been young men, supporting women and children on low-wage jobs. Many of the dead were the sole breadwinners for families in New York and overseas, where they sent portions of their monthly paychecks. A typical scenario following the fire saw a lone woman supporting her family on a meager welfare payment. The city advised widows to seek help from the Crime Victims Board to replace the money brought in by deceased husbands. Often, though, these men had been employed in insecure jobs where they were paid cash under the table, so there was no paperwork to prove their claims.

Men who survived but who had lost children or wives could also struggle financially as a result of the fire. In the wake of the tragedy, private lawyers who were eager to profit from service fees made audacious claims to surviving relatives on the probability of successful litigation against the owners: they would surely pay "dearly and quickly," but as we have seen, there was a long lag between the fire and the finalization of the case against DiLorenzo, Weiss and Jaffe. In the meantime, lured by the promises and naive about the workings of the legal system, many quit their jobs and found themselves broke and unable to support their families.

In some cases where relatives would otherwise have been able to go to work, they were so crippled by depression, PTSD and other mental health conditions following the fire that they were incapable.

Alba Bulnes lost her son in the fire, but her husband survived. Even so, he was unable to work. She described how he retreated into himself in the deepest depression.

"He was in a stage that he didn't even want to come to the window," said Bulnes's wife, Alba, who has been through her own bout of depression. "He would just stay in the bedroom, or walk from the bedroom to the living room, from the living room to the kitchen."

* * *

Firefighters and EMS personnel involved in dealing with the aftermath of the fire also had had a long journey ahead of them in coming to terms with what had happened, even though they were experienced in dealing with tragedies. Some left service altogether after Happy Land. They had never witnessed anything like it, and they never wanted to see anything similar again. For them, no matter their level of commitment, or whatever solid benefits they enjoyed as part of their jobs, it simply wasn't worth it anymore.

Firefighter Dan Cronin was 60 years old and a year away from retirement when the Happy Land fire took place. He told his daughter, writer and teacher Mary Cronin, that it was the worst fire he was ever at.

"That was saying a lot, considering my father spent the bulk of his career in the Bronx, much of it in the South Bronx during the chaotic arson years." Mary said that her father didn't talk too much about what happened at work, so she knew the fire had affected him badly.

Decades later, she searched for photos from the fire online and spotted an image of her father. "In the background of one, I think I see him. But it is in the worst possible instance for a firefighter: the bodies are lined up on the sidewalk. There are no rescues to be made, no lives to save."

For those who left the service, or retired, like Dan Cronin, the Happy Land fire would hopefully become a painful but distant memory. For many of those who stayed, history had a new, unprecedented tragedy in store for them: 9/11. A good number of men who attended the scene at Happy Land were involved in the fire rescue effort at the Twin Towers, and many also died in that catastrophe.

Amongst those who lost their lives in 9/11 was Dennis Devlin. In his last moments before dying when the towers collapsed, Devlin tried to get help for overwhelmed firefighters amid the chaos. Devlin's voice was amongst those heard in the haunting 911 recordings released after the disaster. "We're in a state of confusion," Devlin is heard saying. "We have no cell phone service anywhere."

* * *

For most people affected by the tragedy, the aftermath was overwhelmingly negative. For Garifuna residents of New York, the picture was more mixed. In the short term, as we have seen, the fire had shattered their community. There was barely a Garifuna alive in the city who had not lost someone. And they had also lost the sense of place, camaraderie and belonging that was once provided by the club, no matter how dangerous its environment.

As time passed, however, this event came to constitute a catalytic and galvanizing force in the lives of Garifuna New Yorkers. For one thing, it was not until after the disaster that the mainstream press began to even use the term Garifuna for this ethnic group. There was little consciousness of them as a distinct collective in New York prior to Happy Land. The tragedy became part of Bronx Garifuna lore; it was later referred to as "the Garifuna awakening."

And thereafter, Garifunas in New York began to mobilize to lobby the city to address the specific needs and disadvantages of the group as it struggled to gain recognition and integrate into New York life. The Happy Land fire introduced the Garifuna ethnic group to New York and the world.

In April 1990, at the first mass held commemorating the victims, the Honduran President Rafael Leonardo Callejas spoke and alluded to the need for gathering places for Hondurans to replace dangerous and illegal clubs. Subsequently, with the cooperation of the Catholic Archdiocese of New York and the City, efforts were initiated to develop a cultural and recreation center in the Bronx. Later, in 1992, when the building's owners were fined and ordered to pay compensation, Alexander DiLorenzo agreed to pay $150,000 towards the creation of the center. Mayor David Dinkins also reportedly donated the land for the center.

The plan to create the center was spearheaded by the Federation of Honduran Organizations of New York—an umbrella organization of various Honduran groups in New York—which was created in response to the Happy Land Social Club Fire. Unfortunately the organization faltered and disbanded over time, and the new administration Mayor Rudy Giuliani swept in in 1994 was not amenable to its plans and interests. The center was never built.

Dinkins's war on illegal clubs was only partially successful. After an intense crackdown in the two months following the fire, the administration wound back the size of the Social Club Task Force by half, and operations were lightened. Soon, as in years past, the old pattern re-emerged: clubs that were closed down tended to just reopen again later or crop up at new locations.

The powerful, shocking image of the Happy Land fire, however, had been burned into the public's mind. Mayor Rudy Giuliani would seize upon that, as well as the multi-agency institutional task force set-up created by Dinkins in the wake of the fire, to achieve the results that his predecessor couldn't. His administration presided over a period in which New York became almost unrecognizable from the city of the Dinkins era—and during which its nightlife was almost completely decimated.

Dinkins had been somewhat inhibited in his efforts by his desire to please liberal-leaning and minority constituents. Giuliani didn't care about any of that. His vision of New York and its public spaces was as a safe, clean and orderly city that catered to families, tourists and white people with money, and he was going to achieve it against any and all opposition.

He implemented that vision by restoring the operation of the antiquated cabaret law, which decreed that there couldn't be more than three people dancing in one space without a cabaret license. Cabaret licenses were expensive and difficult to obtain. Police began making "quality of life" raids and issuing club owners with infringements for dancing, smoking, exit lights, building code violations—just about anything they could find. The fines crippled club owners financially and forced them to close. The new beefed-up police forces with their zero-tolerance policies, on the ground day and night in every borough of New York, took over the previously futile role of building inspectors in controlling the clubs, and that short-circuited the miscommunication and lack of follow-up between agencies.

Some illegal clubs still persisted by virtue of the fact that they completely concealed their operation and hid themselves from scrutiny in the way that Happy Land had done. But most clubs that didn't have the money to meet the strict new standards simply vanished. In their place were the new "lounges"— places which were, as *Vice* writer Michael Musto put it, "virtually dance-free venues where you sat and got rigor mortis as you tried to scream over Top 40 songs, hip-hop, and dance-pop."

Immigrant residents in the Bronx weren't, at this time, too concerned about the closure of social clubs. While all this was going on, police were coming right into people's homes to conduct raids. The period saw a wave of no-knock wrong-address raids on black and Latino homes across the city, in which the apartments of unoffending citizens were ransacked and children were menaced at gunpoint. Paramilitary NYPD "anti-drug" operations terrorized whole communities in Brooklyn and the Bronx.

It was often said at the time that for anyone who wasn't a white yuppie, life in New York resembled living under a police state. But, amongst all the fervor to stamp out crime, clean away the graffiti and make the homeless disappear, for the first time in a long time, regulations enforcing building and fire safety were being passed and enforced with zeal.

It was part of the "broken windows" philosophy that neoconservative criminologists adopted in the seventies and eighties, and which inspired Giuliani's vision for New York. The idea was that a single broken window might inspire criminals to break more windows. As criminologist James Q. Wilson wrote, "If the windows are not repaired, the tendency is for vandals to break a few more windows. Eventually, they may even break into the building, and if it's unoccupied, perhaps become squatters or light fires inside. Or consider a pavement. Some litter accumulates. Soon, more litter accumulates. Eventually, people even start leaving bags of refuse from take-out restaurants there or even break into cars..." Small, visible signs of neglect and disorder must be eradicated to prevent further crime and disorder. Neglected, dirty, unsafe buildings were on Giuliani's target list.

The next decade saw a steep reduction in the number of fatal fires across the city, whether in clubs or other kinds of commercial or residential premises. Nobody wanted another Happy Land, and the new enthusiasm for regulation, policing and surveillance in New York meant that chaos, disorder and crime of all kinds was on the decline.

As Tony Saporito wrote for the *Commercial Observer*, "Happy Land forever changed our city's building codes, as well as its health and safety laws, helping to make our homes, workplaces, and public establishments significantly safer. In 2016, New York City documented 48 fire deaths, the lowest number in the Fire Department of the City of New York's 100 years of recordkeeping. The steady decline in fire deaths over the past decades can be directly traced to new and strengthened safety laws and regulations."

In the Bronx, in the years since Happy Land there has been increasing vigilance applied in terms of codes, regulations and inspections to prevent another tragedy. Ivine Galarza, district manager of Community Board 6, where Happy Land operated, dubbed March "Fire Prevention and Safety Month" in her community to remind those of the lives lost in that blaze. "If they can get away with it, believe me, they will," she said of club operators. "Most of them [in the Bronx] are up to code because we are vigilant."

"People who own clubs want to make as much money as they can and they will put people in danger," said NYPD Deputy Inspector William McSorley, who has been inspecting clubs for the past 10 years and says he comes across many repeat offenders. McSorley, commanding officer of the 48th Precinct, cites overcrowding as a major problem in Bronx clubs. "The reason why we have so many rules and regulations is because of tragedies," he said. "They don't see the potential problems by having too many people in a club or not having a fire door or security—they look at it as losing money by not letting everyone in." Galarza said the inspections are "an ongoing process" that will continue. "Everyone wants to be safe and make certain where they go won't turn into another Happy Land situation."

In 2016, a devastating fire broke out at an illegal warehouse party in Oakland, San Francisco—a fire that drew many comparisons to Happy Land. The Ghost Ship was an artists' collective which on the night in question was hosting a rave party featuring deejays and producers from the house music record label 100% Silk. Like the building that housed the Happy Land club, the warehouse was a fire-trap and a disaster waiting to happen. It lacked permits for residential and entertainment uses, and the interior was a snaking maze of makeshift corridors and spaces created from the erection of piles of highly flammable junk including furniture, pianos, art, and mannequins, most of which were made of wood. The building had no sprinklers or smoke detectors, and only one functional stairway to the upper floor, which was constructed out of stacks of wood pallets. The alternative second floor stairway was concealed behind piles of contents and furnishings.

There were about fifty people in the building on the night of the fire. Those who escaped were on the lower floor and had to crawl on hands and knees under the smoke through the maze of clutter to find the front door, the sole exit. Most on the second floor had no way out as the pallet-staircase was on fire. The fire was thought to have begun with an electrical malfunction, but nobody knows for sure as the damage to the interior of the warehouse made proper investigation of the causes impossible.

Ghost Ship's master tenant Derick Almena and his assistant Max Harris were arrested and charged with felony involuntary manslaughter in connection with the fire. But some commentators and even survivors said the result was a little unfair, even if legally it made perfect sense. Why? They pointed out that due to gentrification and skyrocketing rents in San Francisco, unsafe warehouse buildings such as Ghost Ship were the only places that low-income artists could afford to live, especially when they needed to remain close to central areas of the city for their work. Almena had been doing the people a favor by giving them a place to live and work.

The Oakland warehouse fire, like the Happy Land tragedy, is a reminder that low-income and marginal people are often the most vulnerable to disaster risks because they often don't have the funds, resources and civic recognition to enable them to occupy safe and compliant spaces, whether for living or recreation. Later tragedies such as the Grenfell Tower fire have proved the same point again.

* * *

Today, where Happy Land once stood, the bland facade of a Western Union branch yields no hint of the music, the dancing, and the memories both good and bad. But the pink obelisk memorial to the 87, still collecting flowers and tokens all these years later, and the annual processions in remembrance of the dead and the sufferings of their loved ones, are a timeless testament to the enduring and indelible significance of this event for the Central American communities of the Bronx.

While the painful memories linger, much else has changed in the Bronx. At the time of writing, the unthinkable has happened: the Bronx has begun to gentrify. The former blighted South Bronx has earned a new moniker amongst real estate professionals: "So-Bro," suggestive of a ritzy Manhattan neighborhood. Wealthy white professionals are increasingly buying up Bronx apartments and properties and driving the real estate market up. And the old corner stores with affordable groceries and products for poor locals are increasingly replaced by boutiques and expensive chain retailers.

For lifelong Bronx resident Leette Eaton-White, the first obvious sign of her neighborhood's transformation came at the local supermarket. There on a shelf the 31-year old college administrator noticed Method, an organic (and relatively pricey) line of cleaning products. "I had only seen them in Manhattan or Westchester previously. I instantly thought, 'Oh no, this is the beginning of the end,'" White said. She added that "prices for everything [in the area] have gone up. Even though income hasn't changed much, the cost living gets higher all the time."

The changes have led many longer-term residents, including those who lived through Happy Land, to feel fearful of the future as they get priced out of their old home. And once again, many Hondurans, Puerto Ricans and Mexicans who lived in the area for years, who came to the United States in search of a home, are packing up and leaving. As the Bronx was one of the few remaining affordable boroughs in New York, often this means heading for the outskirts, or for other cities altogether. But it seems that in early twentieth-century America, a place of growing inequality, the places left to go are dwindling.

A poem by Wing Pang aptly describes the immigrant experience one of potential perpetual motion and rootlessness:

We carry tears in our eyes: good-bye father, good-bye mother
We carry soil in small bags: may home never fade in our hearts
We carry names, stories, memories of our villages, fields, boats
We carry scars from proxy wars of greed
We carry carnage of mining, droughts, floods, genocides
We carry dust of our families and neighbors incinerated in mushroom clouds
We carry our islands sinking under the sea
We carry our hands, feet, bones, hearts and best minds for a new life...
We carry old homes along the spine, new dreams in our chests
We carry yesterday, today and tomorrow.

Many from the immigrant communities of the Bronx are embarking again, just as they did years ago, on journeys in search of an affordable and welcoming home that seems increasingly elusive.

Pushed to the margins of life, they are once again on the move, drifting outwards into the uncertain future.

Dear reader,

We hope you enjoyed reading *Happy Land*. Please take a moment to leave a review in Amazon, even if it's a short one. Your opinion is important to us.

Discover more books by OJ Modjeska at https://www.nextchapter.pub/authors/oj-modjeska

Want to know when one of our books is free or discounted for Kindle? Join the newsletter at http://eepurl.com/bqqB3H

Best regards,

OJ Modjeska and the Next Chapter Team

You might also like:
A City Owned by OJ Modjeska

To read the first chapter for free, please head to:
https://www.nextchapter.pub/books/a-city-owned

About the Author

OJ Modjeska is a historian, criminologist, and author. She graduated from the University of Sydney with a PhD in modern American history in 2004 and received her graduate diploma in criminology from Sydney Law School in 2015. In 2015 she was awarded the JH McClemens Memorial Prize by Sydney Law School for her scholarship in criminology. Before pursuing a writing career, she worked for many years as a legal writer and editor. OJ writes books of narrative non-fiction true crime and disaster analysis. Previous bestsellers include "Gone: Catastrophe in Paradise" and the two-part true crime series "Murder by Increments." If you enjoy this book and would like to receive news of new releases, consider subscribing to her mailing list at the link below.

http://ojmodjeska.blogspot.com.au
www.estoire.co